# Table of Contents

**1.** What Is a Community? **2**

**2.** Visiting an Urban Community **4**

**3.** Visiting a Rural Community **6**

**4.** Services **8**

**5.** Maps and How to Use Them **10**

**6.** How We Use Our Land **12**

**7.** Buying and Selling **14**

**8.** Transportation **18**

**9.** A Changing Community **20**

**10.** Cultural Communities **22**

**11.** Forestry and Mining **26**

**12.** Farming and Fishing **30**

**13.** Cities in Ontario **34**

**14.** Greater Toronto Area **38**

**15.** Moving to Halifax **42**

**16.** Provinces and Territories **44**

**17.** Environment: Land **46**

**18.** Environment: Air **48**

**19.** Environment: Water **50**

**20.** In Our Own Backyard **53**

**21.** Comparing Our Communities **55**

All terms appearing in boldfaced type in the text are defined in the Glossary on pages 62 to 64.

Refer to the inside back cover for a full map of Ontario showing a variety of communities, including those featured in the text.

D1529200

Sintra and Kinzie are cousins. Both live in Ontario. Sintra lives in Toronto. Kinzie lives in Grey County, just outside Hanover. They are planning to visit each other in the summer.

Grandpa Shastri is a truck driver. He lives in Ottawa but drives his truck all over Ontario and other parts of Canada.

**Dear Sintra and Kinzie,**

Your parents told me that you're going to visit each other this summer. What a great idea! You'll learn a lot about living in the city and in the country. Kinzie, I hear that you are going to Toronto in July. Sintra, I hear you will be in Grey County in August.

Your visits remind me of a story I know. It is called *Town Mouse, Country Mouse*. In the story, the town mouse and the country mouse visit each other. They learn a lot about each other's lives. What things do you think will be different about the places where each of you live? What will be the same?

I'm glad to hear that you want to learn about different communities. In fact, I have a great idea. I will send you letters and pictures as I'm driving my truck across Canada this summer. I visit lots of different places!

**Love,
Grandpa Shastri**

### DID YOU KNOW?

Country is another word for an area outside the city.

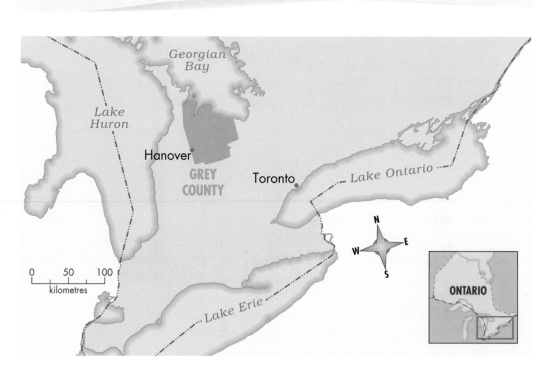

This map shows Toronto, where Sintra lives, and Grey County, where Kinzie lives.

## WHAT IS A COMMUNITY?

A **community** is a group of people who share common interests and experiences. The members of a community often live or work in the same area.

Communities can be small or very large. Your family, for example, is your closest and most personal community. It is a very small community. Your school is also a community. The students, teachers, and other staff in your school are part of the school community.

Your town or city is a community, too. It is a larger community than your school, with many more people.

## WHAT MAKES A GOOD COMMUNITY?

We all want our community to be a good place for everyone. A good community is one that is friendly, safe, and clean.

*A crossing guard helps children to cross the street safely. Does your community have a crossing guard to help you cross the street?*

### A Good Community Is...

**Friendly:** In a friendly community, everyone feels welcome. Nobody is left out, and people help one another.

**Safe:** In a safe community, people follow rules. That way, they don't get hurt when they are working and playing.

**Clean:** In a clean community, people don't litter. They try to look after their **environment**—the land, air, and water. They recycle to help keep the environment clean.

**Urban or Rural**
- number of people
- use of land

**Location**
- where it is
- why people live there

**DESCRIBING A COMMUNITY**

**Community Life**
- jobs
- recreation

**Natural Environment**
- how people use and protect their environment

*In this book, you will learn about many different communities in Ontario and across Canada. This diagram shows key things you will learn along with Grandpa Shastri, Sintra, and Kinzie.*

### SOMETHING TO DO

1. Read the book *Town Mouse, Country Mouse* by Jan Brett. Is your community like the one the country mouse lives in? Or is it more like the one the town mouse lives in? Explain your answer.

2. Make a poster that shows students in your school how to make your school or neighbourhood a better community.

Hi, my name is Sintra. I live in an area of Toronto called East York. This is an older part of the city. It has many houses and a few small apartments. Many people live close to one another. There is also a big park called Taylor Creek Park.

The houses on my street are small. They are built close together. There are 64 houses on my short street! I live in a 75-year-old house that is semi-detached. Semi-detached means that two houses are joined together.

Our house is near the Chester subway station. A subway is a train that runs underground. We often ride it to go shopping and visit friends. We also live close to my school and the library.

I live with my mom, dad, grandma, and little sister, Kaye. She is 4 and I am 8. My mom is a Grade 3 teacher. My dad is a musician. He has a room in our house where he plays and records his music.

I have two best friends. One of them is Ping, and the other is my cousin Kinzie. Ping lives in a high-rise building not too far from my house. A high-rise is a tall building with many apartments. Kinzie lives near a small town called Hanover.

This summer, Kinzie and I are going to visit each other. She will spend a week at my house, and I will spend a week at hers. My mom said that I could plan the things I want to show Kinzie during the week. I have lots of ideas!

## DID YOU KNOW?

The number of people living in Toronto, or its **population**, is 2.5 million.

## What Does Urban Mean?

There are different types of communities. In an **urban community**, many people live close together. We often call urban communities towns and cities. A **town** is a small urban community. A **city** is a large urban community.

### Sintra's Urban Community

## SINTRA'S PLAN

**Sunday**

A.M.: Kinzie arrives with her family!

P.M.: Walk around my neighbourhood, and go to Taylor Creek Park to play.

**Monday**

A.M.: Take the subway downtown, and go up the CN Tower.

P.M.: Have lunch in Chinatown, and go shopping.

**Tuesday**

A.M.: Go for a walk in the Beaches.

P.M.: Go to Walter Stewart Library to take part in the summer kids' reading program.

**Wednesday**

A.M.: Take the ferry to Centre Island for a picnic.

Late P.M.: Go to hear Dad's jazz band play at Harbourfront.

**Thursday**

A.M.: Spend the morning at Ping's apartment.

P.M.: Visit the Royal Ontario Museum with Ping and his mom.

**Friday**

A.M.: Go to the Toronto Zoo. Spend all day! Ride a camel!

P.M.: Have dinner at our favourite Trinidadian restaurant on the Danforth.

**Saturday**

A.M.: Go to my school playground to play.

P.M.: Kinzie and her family go home.

*The city of Toronto, where you can see the CN Tower*

*A subway*

*Chinatown*

*From these photos, what can you say about a place that is urban? For example, what can you say about its buildings, how people get around, its streets, and the number of people who live here?*

## SOMETHING TO DO

1. Imagine that you have a cousin or friend coming to stay with you for a week. Create your own plan like Sintra's. Which places do you like to visit? Which ones will you visit with your cousin or friend?

2. Write a letter telling your cousin or friend about the plans that you have made from activity 1.

3. Sintra lives in a semi-detached house. What other kinds of homes are found in urban communities? Draw or cut out pictures of homes, and create a picture dictionary describing them.

Hi, my name is Kinzie. I live in Grey County, Ontario. It is a rural community. I go to school in a nearby town called Hanover. That's also where we do most of our shopping.

My house used to be a one-room school. My parents turned it into a home. The stone part of the building is over 100 years old. We have big gardens and a lot of trees.

I live with my mom, dad, and 2-year-old brother, Joseph. We have a dog named Pepper and a cat named Kendal. My dad is a veterinarian. That's an animal doctor. Sometimes he looks after dogs and cats, but he also looks after cows, pigs, and sheep. My mom is an airplane pilot. She works at the Saugeen Municipal Airport near Hanover.

Houses are spaced far apart where I live. I can see only a few other homes down the road from my house. We like to walk down the road to visit our neighbours. We also walk to the lake at the end of our road. Most of the time, we drive to get around. I take a bus to and from school.

Most of our neighbours are dairy and beef farmers. Dairy farmers keep cows that give us milk. Beef farmers keep cows that are made into meat. My best friend, Steve, lives on a dairy farm near our place.

My other best friend is my cousin Sintra. She lives in Toronto. She and her family are visiting us this summer. I'm going to show her all my favourite places. I can hardly wait!

## Kinzie's Rural Community

### DID YOU KNOW?

The population of Hanover is 6869.

### What Does Rural Mean?

In a **rural community,** a few people live spread out over a large area. Sometimes a few homes are grouped together in a rural community. These places are called **hamlets** and **villages**. In rural communities, some people work in jobs related to farming, forestry, mining, and fishing.

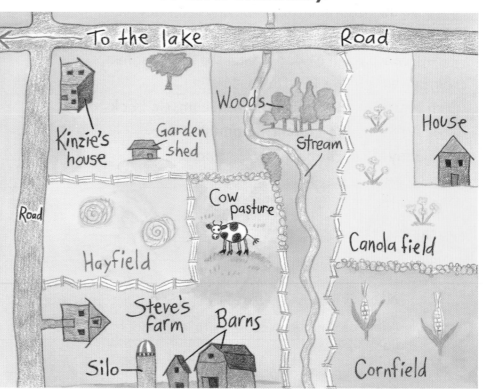

*How are Kinzie's house and street like or different from Sintra's?*

# Visiting a Rural Community

## KINZIE'S PLAN

**Sunday**

P.M.: Sintra and her family arrive from Toronto. Walk to the lake at the end of our road (about 2 km) for canoeing.

**Monday**

A.M.: Visit our neighbour Steve at his family's dairy farm.

P.M.: Play at water park in Chesley (nearby town).

**Tuesday**

A.M.: Hike the trail just outside Hanover. Have a picnic lunch.

P.M.: Have a campfire at home. Sleep over in our tent in the backyard.

**Wednesday**

A.M.: Go to the Hanover Library for the summer kids' reading program.

P.M.: See some animals at Dad's veterinary clinic.

**Thursday**

A.M.: Build a fort in our backyard. Have lunch in the restaurant at the Saugeen Airport.

P.M.: Go swimming at the Hanover Aquatic Centre.

**Friday**

A.M.: Spend the day in Goderich. Go to the beach in the morning. Have lunch at Grandma's.

P.M.: Visit the Huron County Museum. Go back to the beach at sunset to hear the pipe band.

**Saturday**

A.M.: Take the canoe out on the lake again.

P.M.: Sintra and her family go home to Toronto.

*The town of Hanover*

*A rural road*

*A dairy farm in Grey County*

*Look at the photos of Toronto again on page 5. How are the houses and other buildings different from the ones in these photos? How are the rural roads different from urban streets? In what other ways are the two places different and alike?*

## SOMETHING TO DO

1. The girls have planned to do many things on their visits. Make a Venn diagram showing the activities you think are similar and different in the rural and the urban communities.

2. Make a map of the area around your home. Do you live in an urban or a rural community? What features make it urban or rural?

## Dear Sintra and Kinzie,

Thank you for sending me the plans for your visits. Your ideas sound like fun! It might be a good idea to share some information about your communities before your visits. What services do you have in your community? How do you travel within and outside your community? Why do you travel outside your community? Let me know what you find out.

**Love,
Grandpa Shastri**

*Both urban and rural communities have mail service. How are these services different? How are they the same?*

## WHAT ARE SERVICES?

**Services** are things people do for others in their communities. For example, people such as teachers, firefighters, police officers, and mail carriers provide a service to us. Sintra and Kinzie have created charts showing the important services in their communities.

| Sintra's Urban Community: East York, Toronto | |
|---|---|
| **Services** | **My Community Has** |
| education | • my school<br>• a library |
| safety, health, and welfare | • a fire hall<br>• the Toronto Police Service<br>• a big hospital called the Toronto East General<br>• my doctor and dentist<br>• garbage pickup. Garbage is picked up from the end of our driveway once a week.<br>• mail service. Mail is put into our mailbox every weekday. When I want to send a letter, I walk down the street and put it in the big mailbox. |
| shopping | • many kinds of stores, malls, and supermarkets where we buy clothes, books, food, and many other things |
| transportation | • roads for cars<br>• buses and subways to travel within the city<br>• trains and buses to go out of the city<br>• a large airport and some small airports in Toronto |

Rural communities are closely connected to nearby urban communities. For example, Kinzie goes to Hanover regularly to attend school and to visit the library. Although people in urban communities depend on rural areas for things such as food, they don't need to visit rural communities regularly.

## Kinzie's Rural Community: Grey County, Near Hanover

| Services | My Community Has | Hanover Has |
|---|---|---|
| education | • school bus service to my school in Hanover | • my school<br>• a public library |
| safety, health, and welfare | • volunteer firefighters<br>• Ontario Provincial Police<br>• ambulances to take people to the hospital in Hanover<br>• garbage pickup. Garbage is picked up at the end of our lane once a week.<br>• mail service. Mail is put in our mailbox at the end of our lane every weekday. To send a letter, I put it into our mailbox. | • my doctor and dentist<br>• a hospital. This hospital in Hanover is the closest to us. |
| shopping | • farms. We sometimes buy some food from our neighbours. | • many stores |
| transportation | • roads. Some roads are paved. Others are gravel.<br>• Saugeen Municipal Airport | • a bus that goes to the airports in Toronto and London |

## Why We Visit...

**Rural Communities**
• to ski in winter
• to hike in spring, summer, fall
• to camp in spring and summer
• to buy fresh produce at farms
• to visit relatives and friends

**Urban Communities**
• to go to big hospitals
• to take planes from big airports
• to take trains
• to shop at different stores
• to visit relatives and friends

### DID YOU KNOW?

In some rural areas, there are no paid firefighters. Adults in the community volunteer. They are trained by professional firefighters.

## SOMETHING TO DO

1. Make a Venn diagram with the headings Urban Services, Rural Services, and Both. Use information from Sintra's and Kinzie's charts to complete the diagram.

2. What are some reasons you might visit a rural or an urban community? Make a list. Compare it to Sintra's or Kinzie's list.

**Dear Sintra and Kinzie,**

Before you learn about different communities in Ontario and the rest of Canada, you need to learn about maps. I am sending you some road maps with this letter. Can you find your communities on these maps?

There are different types of maps. **Road maps** show highways and main roads between communities. **Street maps** show a small area within a community. They help us to find town or city streets, schools, hospitals, and parks. **Physical maps** show lakes, rivers, hills, mountains, and valleys. These are called **physical features**. What other information do you think you can learn from maps?

**Love,**
**Grandpa Shastri**

## How to Make a Map

**Legend**

🛒 Grocery store

Ⓗ Hospital

📷 Library

▭ Park

⛪ Place of worship

🏫 School

Here are some features to include when you make a map.

1. Symbols
   A **symbol** is a picture, colour, shape, or line on a map. Each symbol stands for something, such as a building, water, or a road.

2. Legend
   A **legend** is a list of the symbols on a map. It tells what the symbols mean.

3. Compass Rose
   A **compass rose** is a symbol used on a map that shows the directions north, south, east, and west. These directions are called **cardinal points**. Look at Sintra's map on page 11. To go from her house to school, Sintra travels up the map, along Daisy Road. Since the compass rose shows north is at the top of the map, Sintra travels north.

4. Scale
   A map is smaller than the real place or area it shows. A **scale** is the bar on a map that looks like a ruler. It tells you how far the distances really are and the real size of things. For example, five centimetres on a map might equal one kilometre in real life.

N
W——E
S

0    15    30
metres

# Maps and How to Use Them

## Sintra's Urban Community

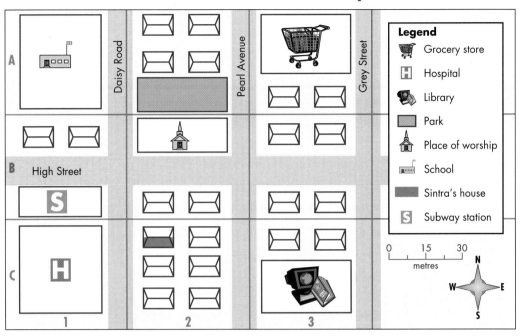

### Legend
- 🛒 Grocery store
- Ⓗ Hospital
- 📖 Library
- ▭ Park
- ⛪ Place of worship
- 🏫 School
- ▭ Sintra's house
- Ⓢ Subway station

0   15   30
metres

N W E S

## Kinzie's Rural Community

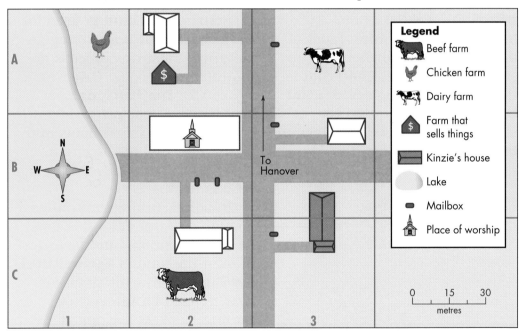

To Hanover

### Legend
- 🐄 Beef farm
- 🐔 Chicken farm
- 🐄 Dairy farm
- $ Farm that sells things
- ▭ Kinzie's house
- 〰 Lake
- ▬ Mailbox
- ⛪ Place of worship

0   15   30
metres

N W E S

## How to Use a Grid

Look at Sintra's map. It is covered in a pattern of lines called a **grid**. There are letters and numbers written around the edges of the grid. They help us find places on the map.

For example, Sintra's house is found at C2. Put your left finger on the letter C and your right finger on the number 2. Slide your left finger across the grid along the squares of C. At the same time, slide your right finger up the grid along the squares of 2. When your fingers meet, they should both point to Sintra's house.

This letter-number combination (C2) that we use to locate a place is called a **coordinate**.

## SOMETHING TO DO

1. By sliding your fingers along the grid, find and name the places at the following coordinates on both Sintra's and Kinzie's maps: A1, C1, and C3. Now give the coordinates for the following places on each map: the girl's house, a place of worship, and a place that sells food.

2. Look at Kinzie's map. Using cardinal points, give the direction (north, south, east, or west) that Kinzie travels to go from home to the lake. What direction does she travel to go from home to school? From school to home?

**Dear Sintra and Kinzie,**

You did a great job drawing maps of your neighbourhoods! I saw some interesting differences on your maps. Sintra's street map shows many houses built close together. Nearby is a store, a school, and a library. Kinzie's map shows just a few houses, and each one is far apart from the others. Nearby is mainly farmland.

What do these differences tell us? Rural and urban communities use land in different ways. What else can you find out about how urban and rural communities use their land?

**Love,
Grandpa Shastri**

## USES OF LAND

In urban communities, most of the land is used for homes, stores, and offices. Land that is used for housing is **residential land**. Land that is used for stores and offices is **commercial land**.

Some urban land is used for **industrial buildings**, such as factories. Factories process or manufacture goods. Other land is used for **institutional buildings**. These are public buildings, such as schools and hospitals. Look at the circle graph to see how else urban land is used.

In some rural communities, a small amount of land is used for homes, stores, and factories. A lot of the land is **agricultural land** used for farming. Other land is used for forestry or mining. Look at the box at the top of page 13 to see how the uses of land in rural communities can affect where people work.

Both rural and urban communities keep some areas, such as parks, for recreation. **Recreation** is an activity that is done for fun, such as walking, swimming, skiing, canoeing, or camping.

*This circle graph, also called a pie graph, shows how urban land is used. What takes up the biggest amount of land?*

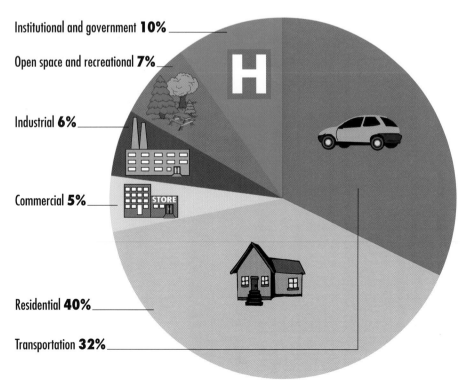

Institutional and government **10%**

Open space and recreational **7%**

Industrial **6%**

Commercial **5%**

Residential **40%**

Transportation **32%**

## Where People Work in Rural Communities

Even though mining, forestry, and farming use a lot of land, not many people work in these jobs. Fewer people are needed in these jobs than in the past because of new machines. Now, most rural people work in jobs where they make things (manufacturing), sell things, or help people (services). Some of these jobs may be connected to mining, forestry, or farming. For example, local businesses may sell farm equipment or manufacture paper from wood.

## THE NATURAL ENVIRONMENT

Most urban and rural communities developed because of useful features in their natural environment. Some of these are
- good soil for farmland
- rivers to provide water power
- lakes and rivers for transportation by boats and large ships
- natural resources, such as forests to log
- land that is not too rocky or hilly for building roads or railway tracks
- lakes or flat land for landing airplanes
- natural areas, such as ponds, rivers, lakes, and forests, that people visit for local recreation or while on their holidays

*Ecotourism allows tourists to visit, enjoy, and learn about wildlife and plants in their natural environment. Rural Ontario has many provincial parks and conservation areas. These areas are set aside to protect plants, wildlife, lakes, and rivers.*

## How We Use the Land as Tourists

**Tourists** are people who travel to other places to spend their holidays. **Tourism** is a business that helps people who are visiting a community. It provides campsites, hotels, restaurants, transportation, shops, and events.

## SOMETHING TO DO

1. How is land used in the area around your school? Draw a map of your school and the road it is on (see Sintra's and Kinzie's maps on page 11). Show the land in the surrounding area. Use symbols on your map to show what the land is used for.

2. How does the natural environment affect your community? Are there natural resources? Rich soil for farms? Rivers for electricity? Flat land for building roads, railway tracks, or an airport? Water for ships? With a partner, create a collage to show the natural environment around your community.

3. Imagine that you are creating a new park for your province. Think of a name for it. Draw a map of the things you want in it (for example, lakes, forests, campsites, places for boats, hiking or ski trails). Look up the Ontario Parks Web site (www.ontarioparks.com) or get pamphlets about Ontario Parks to help you.

**Dear Sintra and Kinzie,**

You asked me to tell you more about my job and why I visit so many communities. I work for a company that makes canned foods. I drive a large truck. I take canned fruits and vegetables from a factory to communities across Canada.

The factory is in a town. The fruits and vegetables, such as pears, tomatoes, and beans, come from farms in rural communities around the town. Urban and rural communities are connected by things we buy from, and sell to, one another.

When people buy and sell things, we call it trade. What things can you buy in your community? Where do you buy them? Which communities have they come from?

**Love,
Grandpa Shastri**

## WHAT IS TRADE?

**Trade** is the buying or selling of goods and services. Trade can take place among members of a community, or it can take place between communities. Today, when we trade, we usually use money.

**Goods** are products that are produced or manufactured. These can be things we *need* to survive, such as food, clothing, and clean water. Goods can also be things we *want*, such as toys, video games, and books.

Services are things people do for others. People such as doctors, plumbers, and teachers help make our communities and lives better.

*This is one way that we trade—money in exchange for bread. Someone who buys goods or services is a* **consumer**.

Sometimes people provide both goods and services. For example, a pizza restaurant sells pizza (a good) and also delivers it to your door (a service). Can you think of other examples where someone provides both goods and services?

## HOW DID TRADE BEGIN?

Communities all over the world have traded for a very long time.

Aboriginal peoples in Canada carried corn, wild rice, meat, fish, furs, and even canoes long distances to exchange with neighbouring communities. This system of trading some goods (such as corn) for other goods (such as canoes) is called the **barter system**.

*Aboriginal peoples brought their furs to a fur trading post like this one to trade with Europeans.*

## WHY IS TRADE IMPORTANT?

### Trade Helps to Build Communities

Trade is important because it brings people together. It helps communities to grow. Aboriginal peoples traded with one another. Later, the first Europeans who came to Canada settled in places where they could trade with the Aboriginal peoples for furs and other goods.

People settled where they could produce goods to trade. For example, farming communities grew in areas where the soil was fertile for growing crops. Some crops, such as grains, were made into flour. The flour was then used to make foods, such as bread. Changing crops into foods is called **processing**.

Communities also started in places that had important natural resources. **Natural resources** are things produced by nature that are useful, such as trees. Trees provide wood for building. **Minerals**, such as iron and gold, are natural resources found in rocks. They provide materials to make tools and jewellery. Changing resources, such as wood or minerals, into things that people use is called **manufacturing**.

Some communities grew where there was a river. The river provided the power needed to run mills. There was no electricity long ago, so the **mills** used moving water to turn large grinding and cutting machines.

*Hamilton is on the shores of Lake Ontario. Communities often developed along main **transportation routes**, such as lakes, rivers, and railroad lines. These routes made it easier to move goods and people.*

## QUICK DEFINITIONS

**Industry** is the business of processing or manufacturing goods. A **factory** is a place where goods are processed or manufactured. The goods are then taken to a store.

### Trade Provides Jobs

People in a community work at jobs to make things for trade. For example, a dairy farmer in Huron County (a rural community) makes money by selling milk to a factory in Teeswater (a small town nearby). The factory uses people to drive the trucks that pick up the milk at the farm. The factory also has people who process the milk into cheese, butter, ice cream, or milk that we can drink. The factory sells its products to grocery stores in towns and cities across Ontario. Trucks take the processed products to these stores. The stores hire people to work as cashiers and managers.

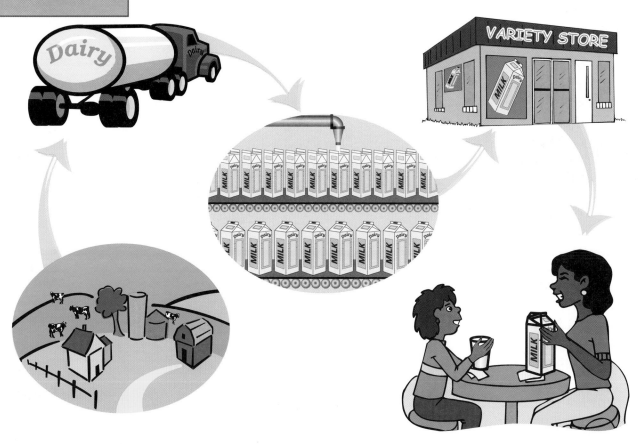

*When you buy milk, you are helping the farmer, the truck driver, the dairy workers, and the grocery-store workers keep their jobs.*

### Trade Helps Communities Grow and Survive

Communities suffer when trade stops. This can happen when transportation routes, factories, or natural resources disappear. For example, if train services to a community are cut back, transporting goods would become harder and more expensive. If all the trees in an area are cut down, people in a community that depends on making lumber would lose their jobs. The lumber mills would shut down and let their workers go. These people would not have money to buy things. This would hurt the community's stores. People might leave the community to find work. The community would get smaller and might even disappear.

## TRADE IN ONTARIO

Communities in Ontario trade many different goods and services. Industries in Ontario make the goods that the province trades. The bar graph on the right shows the main industries in Ontario.

Communities in Ontario trade their goods and services with one another. They also trade with other provinces in Canada and with countries around the world.

Selling goods or services to other provinces, territories, or countries is called **exporting**. Buying goods and services from other provinces, territories, or countries is called **importing**.

Look at the table on the right. This table shows some of the goods and services Ontario exports to other provinces and territories. It also shows what important goods and services Ontario imports from other provinces and territories.

## TRADE CONNECTS PEOPLE

Trade is a large web that connects us all. It is what allows us to produce and share all of the things we need. Which places across Canada and around the world is your community connected to?

### Main Industries in Ontario, 2001

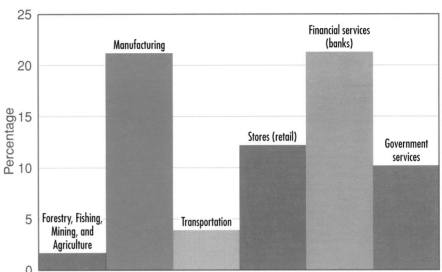

Source: Ontario Ministry of Finance, June 2002

### Ontario's Top Imports and Exports

| Top Four Ontario Exports | Top Four Ontario Imports |
| --- | --- |
| 1. Cars and car parts | 1. Cars and car parts |
| 2. Machinery and equipment | 2. Machinery and equipment |
| 3. Plastics and plastic items | 3. Scientific equipment |
| 4. Metals | 4. Plastics and plastic items |

Source: Ontario Ministry of Finance, Ontario Fact Sheet, June 2002

## SOMETHING TO DO

1. With a partner or in a small group, list businesses in the community around your school. Make a chart. Put the businesses on the chart under these headings: Provides Mostly Goods, Provides Mostly Services, Provides Goods and Services Equally. You could use a local *Yellow Pages* phone book to help you.

2. A bakery in Ottawa makes muffins. The main ingredients are eggs, butter, maple syrup, wheat flour, oatmeal, milk, and applesauce. Describe where you think these ingredients come from and how you think they get to the bakery. What does this tell you about how rural and urban businesses depend on each other?

## DID YOU KNOW?

Quebec is Ontario's largest provincial trading partner.

**Dear Sintra and Kinzie,**

I got your thank-you notes for the maple syrup I sent you from Quebec. I'm glad you enjoyed it. Did you know that Quebec produces 70 per cent of the world's maple syrup?

You asked some interesting questions about how goods are moved or transported between communities. There are many ways of transporting goods. Transporting by road is one way. Some of the other ways are by air, rail, and water. Moving people from one place to another is also important. What are some of the ways you travel?

**Love,
Grandpa Shastri**

## ROAD

Ontario has many roads and highways. Highway 401 is one of them. It runs from Windsor, Ontario, to Montreal, Quebec. It is part of the Trans-Canada Highway, the longest highway in the world. Today, cars and trucks are the main methods of transportation in Ontario.

In cities, people can take buses to go from one place in the city to another. These buses run throughout the day. There are also buses that travel long distances between cities.

Many small urban and rural communities are not connected by bus at all. Buses that do go from smaller places to cities run less often than city buses. They might run daily or weekly.

Many urban communities and some rural areas provide special vans for people with disabilities.

## AIR

Ontario has over 60 airports. Toronto's Pearson International Airport is the largest in Canada. About 23 million passengers travel through Pearson each year. This airport handles over 400 000 tonnes of goods each year.

Some northern communities can be reached only by air. Air travel is very important in these communities. People and goods, such as food and medical supplies, are transported by air.

*Where Highway 401 passes through Toronto, there are as many as 14 lanes for traffic! This section of the highway is the second most-travelled highway in North America. The only busier one is in California.*

## RAIL

Some people ride on passenger trains, such as VIA Rail, to travel long distances. People who live in communities close to the Greater Toronto Area (GTA) can also travel on the Government of Ontario (GO) trains.

The GTA also has an underground rail system called the subway. Each day, thousands of people use the subway to go to work, shopping centres, and other places. Rural communities used to have trains that connected them, but most passenger trains stopped running when car travel became more popular.

## WATER

In the past, ships could sail on the St. Lawrence River only to Montreal. Beyond that, rapids and waterfalls made travelling dangerous.

In the 1950s, the Canadian government built the St. Lawrence Seaway to make travelling safe. Large ships can now sail past the rapids near Montreal. They can also sail on the Great Lakes. As well, communities on the Great Lakes can ship goods across the Atlantic Ocean to countries around the world.

*Freight trains move goods across North America in the same way that passenger trains move people.*

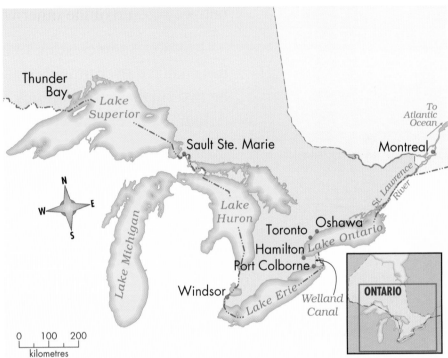

*The St. Lawrence Seaway extends through the Great Lakes and the St. Lawrence River. This map shows the major Canadian ports along this seaway.*

## SOMETHING TO DO

1. Choose one of the methods of transportation discussed in this chapter.
   a) Make a model of a vehicle you would need to travel that way.
   b) Describe ways people in Ontario might use this method of transportation.
2. What are the main methods of transportation in your community? Make a booklet showing the different methods. Give useful information about them (such as where the bus stops near your school or where to find a street map).

### DID YOU KNOW?

In the past, travelling long distances was difficult. Water travel in the winter is still difficult today because of bad weather and ice. The Welland Canal, which connects Lake Ontario and Lake Erie, is open only during the spring, summer, and fall.

**Dear Sintra and Kinzie,**

I'm writing to you from Thunder Bay. This northwestern Ontario city is on Lake Superior, one of the Great Lakes.

Thunder Bay is a large **port** where goods are loaded onto ships and taken to other parts of the world. The Trans-Canada Highway also runs through Thunder Bay. This stretch of the highway is the only major road link between eastern and western Canada.

It is always interesting to learn about how a community has changed over time. For example, Thunder Bay used to be two smaller communities called Fort William and Port Arthur. I am sending you some stories about Thunder Bay.

**Love,**
**Grandpa Shastri**

*This painting shows the Fort William area in 1865.*

**DID YOU KNOW?**

Over many years, old Fort William decayed. In the 1970s, an accurate replica was built nearby. The fort is an important historical site. It is visited by thousands of people each year.

## EARLY ABORIGINAL COMMUNITIES

Aboriginal peoples have lived in the Thunder Bay area for over 11 000 years. The Anishinabe peoples (sometimes called the Ojibwa) were the first to live here. They were hunters. For much of the year, they lived in small family groups. They camped in the woods, following the animals they hunted for food. Their homes were cone-shaped lodges made of a wood frame covered with bark and animal skins.

Aboriginal peoples settled along rivers near Lake Superior because they provided transportation routes. These Aboriginal peoples travelled along the rivers using canoes.

## FUR TRADE

Early Europeans came to Canada looking for furs.

Aboriginal peoples knew how to hunt for and trap animals, such as beavers. They traded furs for European goods.

Since Thunder Bay is close to the middle of Canada, it became an important meeting place for traders from the east and west. Lake Superior also provided a good transportation route to other parts of Canada. Fur companies began building trading posts here. Fort William was the most important trading post in the area.

## FORT WILLIAM AND PORT ARTHUR

After the 1820s, mining became more important than fur trading. Copper and gold were found in the Fort William area. When silver was found in 1870, the community of Port Arthur developed. Both communities also had a forestry industry.

**Legends** are stories that have been passed down from one generation to the next. Some legends are true stories. Others are fictional but tell about important ideas.

### The Legend of the Sleeping Giant

A large rock sits at the end of the Sibley Peninsula in Thunder Bay. It looks like a person sleeping. Aboriginal legend says that it is the sleeping body of Nanabosho (the giant), son of the West Wind. He led his people to the north shore of Lake Superior to save them from enemies.

One day, while sitting by the lake, Nanabosho scratched a rock and discovered silver. He worried that the silver would attract Europeans who would want to take it. He told his people not to tell anyone about this secret. One chief did. Later, Nanabosho saw some Europeans coming in a canoe to find the silver. He created a great storm, drowning the men. The Great Spirit was angry with Nanabosho and turned him into stone.

*Source: Sleeping Giant Provincial Park version, Queen's Printer, 2000*

*The Sleeping Giant as seen from Thunder Bay*

In 1885, the Canadian Pacific Railway was completed. Grain was brought to Fort William by rail from western farms and then shipped across Lake Superior.

In the 1960s, the Trans-Canada Highway was built. This meant that large transport trucks also began to pass through this area.

In 1971, Fort William and Port Arthur joined to form Thunder Bay.

**MODERN THUNDER BAY**

Shipping and forestry are still very important in Thunder Bay. There are now pulp and paper mills, where wood from trees is made into paper.

Thunder Bay has art galleries, museums, theatres, and shopping centres. Nearby provincial parks, such as Sleeping Giant and Kakabeka Falls, attract campers, hikers, and boaters in the summer and skiers in the winter.

*Today more than 100 000 people live in Thunder Bay. Look at this photo closely. How would you say that this city uses its land?*

### SOMETHING TO DO

1. a) What are the four main periods in Thunder Bay's growth described in this chapter? With a partner, create a timeline with descriptions of these periods.

   b) Choose one of the periods. Pretend you are a character living at that time. Write a letter describing your day-to-day life.

2. The legend of the Sleeping Giant is only one of many Aboriginal legends. Find another Aboriginal legend. Share the story with your class in a dramatic presentation or a book report.

**Dear Sintra and Kinzie,**

Often, within a large community, there are smaller communities that share language, ways of living, belief systems, etc. These are called cultural communities. Both urban and rural places have cultural communities.

Members of these cultural communities may live in areas scattered throughout a city or province, or they may live in a neighbourhood of a large city. They often gather together to take part in events or celebrations. They celebrate and share with others the history, music, dance, food, clothing, art, and religion of their heritage.

I am sending you some information about four cultural communities that I recently visited. Remember that these are only a small sample of the many cultural communities in Ontario.

**Love,
Grandpa Shastri**

## QUICK DEFINITIONS

**Heritage** is everything that has been handed down from the past. This includes **culture**—people's beliefs and the way they live their lives, including their clothing, food, celebrations, languages, and music.

*Gerrard India Bazaar*

## CULTURAL COMMUNITIES IN AN URBAN AREA

### Gerrard India Bazaar

The area around Coxwell Avenue and Gerrard Street in Toronto is known as the Gerrard India Bazaar. This smaller community within a large urban one is made up of people who have roots in southern Asia (India, Pakistan, Bangladesh, and Sri Lanka), East Africa, the Caribbean, and South America.

The businesses of Gerrard India Bazaar offer a variety of goods and services that reflect the cultures of the people. Here, you can find grocery shops with fruits and spices from south Asia. There are clothing shops, with beautiful silks and saris, and jewellery shops, with gleaming gold earrings and bangles. Restaurants serve delicious snacks and sweets. Music from India fills this part of Gerrard Street.

People from different parts of Ontario shop at Gerrard India Bazaar for items that cannot be found easily in other communities.

*This photo shows a sari, a type of clothing worn by women from India. It is finely decorated at the end that is draped over a woman's shoulder. Saris are made from the finest silks, cottons, and nylon. They are sometimes richly designed with gold threads, pearls, and beads.*

## Greektown

Greektown is located on a part of Danforth Avenue in Toronto. Here you will find many Greek restaurants as well as grocery stores, bakeries, clothing stores, and churches. There is also a meeting area with a fountain and a statue of Alexander the Great, an important person in Greek history.

Every summer, this community of restaurant and business owners holds a festival called Taste of the Danforth. The restaurant owners set up booths on the sidewalks of Danforth Avenue. The street is closed to vehicles. People wander along the street and sample many different kinds of foods, such as souvlaki (meat barbecued on a thin stick) and baklava (a sweet dessert). The festival is a great way to get people to come out to this community and try new foods. It attracts visitors to a part of the city that they may not usually visit.

*Do you think you would enjoy visiting Greektown in Toronto for Taste of the Danforth?*

## CULTURAL COMMUNITIES IN RURAL AREAS

### Wikwemikong Reserve, Manitoulin Island

Manitoulin Island lies in Lake Huron. Wikwemikong is located on the eastern side of Manitoulin Island. The name Manitoulin means "Land of the Great Spirit" and Wikwemikong means "Bay of Beavers." Manitoulin Island is linked to northern Ontario by a bridge all year. In the summer, tourists can take a car ferry to Manitoulin from Tobermory in southern Ontario.

Wikwemikong is one of several reserves on Manitoulin. A **reserve** is a piece of land set aside by the government for Aboriginal peoples. Wikwemikong Reserve's main settlement is the village of Wikwemikong on Wikwemikong Bay.

Three different Aboriginal peoples live in Wikwemikong: the Anishinabe (Ojibwa), the Odawa, and the Pottawatomi. The community celebrates its Aboriginal cultures and **traditions**—ideas and ways of doing things that are passed on to younger generations.

One of the many cultural celebrations in Wikwemikong is the yearly Wikwemikong Indian Days. This is one of the largest powwows in Ontario. Traditional Aboriginal dancers compete for prizes. The people of Wikwemikong also share their cultures with non-Aboriginal people. These visitors can tour the Aboriginal Heritage Interpretive Centre as well as buy Aboriginal arts and crafts at stores.

Several important Aboriginal Canadian artists come from Wikwemikong, including Daphne Odjig and Leland Bell.

*Belonging by Daphne Odjig. Aboriginal art is a very important part of our cultural heritage in Canada.*

*Aboriginal peoples of the Wikwemikong Reserve gather at a powwow. Dancing, music, eating, and special ceremonies take place at the powwow.*

## Waterloo Region

Many Mennonite people came to the Waterloo region more than 100 years ago. The Mennonites were Christians who came from areas in Germany, Switzerland, France, and Russia. They did not believe in fighting wars. They hoped that in Canada they would be free to practise their religion without being forced into the army.

Some Mennonites wear what we consider modern clothing. Others continue to dress in traditional clothing. For example, the women wear long dresses and bonnets or prayer caps. The men wear dark clothing and hats. Those who dress in traditional clothing are the Amish and Old Order Mennonites.

Many of the Old Order and Amish Mennonites are farmers. Some sell their goods at local markets, such as the St. Jacob's Farmers' Market, or at local events, such as the Elmira Maple Syrup Festival. These markets and events have attracted many visitors to this community.

**DID YOU KNOW?**

The growth of cities such as Kitchener and Waterloo has led to less farmland and busier roads. Some Mennonites are moving to areas where farmland is cheaper and there is less traffic.

*Some Amish and Old Order Mennonites use horses and buggies to get around instead of cars. These people like to keep their lives simple and independent of modern technology.*

## SOMETHING TO DO

1. Research your own or another cultural community. You might want to read books or talk to neighbours or family members.

   a) Use the following headings: Holidays/Festivals, Foods, Clothing, History, Music/Art/Dance/Drama/Literature. Write sentences under each heading describing your findings.

   b) Using pictures and words, make a collage of the community.

2. Compare two of the communities in this chapter using a Venn diagram. How are they alike and different?

**Dear Sintra and Kinzie,**

I just visited some communities where forestry and mining are important industries. Some of these communities are urban, but the forests and minerals are found in rural areas just outside them.

Tourism is also important in some of these communities. The natural environment provides beautiful parks for camping and hiking. There are also rivers and lakes for swimming and boating. Forestry, mining, and tourism developed because of the natural environment in these communities.

Rural and urban communities are neighbours. Think about how they are connected. What would happen to the forestry industry if towns and cities nearby grew? What would happen to towns and cities if nearby mines ran out of minerals or the forests were destroyed?

**Love,**
**Grandpa Shastri**

## QUICK DEFINITIONS

**Forestry** is the cutting down and replanting of trees. Trees are used to make wood products such as paper, boards, or furniture.

When workers dig the ground with machines to find minerals, they are **mining**. Workers separate minerals from the rocks using high heat. This is called **smelting**.

*This collage shows main natural resources.*

Natural resources are things in nature that are useful to people. They are important because they give us what we need to live.

Almost everything we eat, wear, or use is made from some kind of natural resource.

In many communities, natural resources are important because they provide jobs for people. Some people work getting the resources. They mine for gold, nickel, silver, or salt. They drill for oil and gas. They cut down trees.

Other people work by turning these resources into products we can use. They make cars from metal, furniture from wood, and clothing from cotton and wool. Gas and oil are used to run our cars and heat our homes. Materials such as plastic are also made from gas and oil. Ontario has many natural resources.

## WHITE RIVER: FORESTRY

**Population:** 993

**Transportation Routes:** road, rail (passenger), air (water landing), water (river routes)

**Location:** Northwestern Ontario, halfway between Sault Ste. Marie and Thunder Bay

Forestry is the main industry in White River. Trees in nearby forests are cut and sent to a large sawmill, located just outside the town.

The rivers, lakes, and provincial parks around White River make it a popular place for camping and canoeing. White Lake and Obatanga Provincial Parks and Pukaskwa National Park are beautiful places to visit. Campers come to see wildlife, such as moose, loons, and porcupines.

Two serious fires damaged forests in the White River area in 1976 and 1999. Now special signs remind visitors and residents about how to prevent fires. This is very important because both the forestry and recreation industries around White River depend on healthy forests.

**Legend**

🌲 Forestry industry

⚒ Mining industry

White River

Fox Lake Reserve

Lake Superior

Sudbury

Lake Huron

Lake Michigan

Goderich

Lake Ontario

Lake Erie

0    100    200
kilometres

ONTARIO

*This map shows the locations of the forestry and mining communities discussed in this chapter.*

*Logs from a White River forest.*

### DID YOU KNOW?

In 1914, Captain Harry Colebourn stopped in White River. He bought a black bear cub from a hunter and named her Winnie. When he had to go to war, he left the bear in the London Zoo in England. A little boy named Christopher Robin liked to visit her. The boy's father, A.A. Milne, wrote stories about Winnie the Pooh.

*The Big Nickel is a famous landmark in Sudbury. It is located at an old mine. Today, mines use fewer workers because new methods and machines work more quickly. How do you think this has affected Sudbury?*

## DID YOU KNOW?

Nickel is used to make many kinds of metal stronger. Zinc is used to protect steel from rusting. Lead is used in batteries. Silver is used to make jewellery and camera film. Cobalt is used to make magnets. Platinum is used to make jewellery and the parts of cars that clean the cars' exhaust. Gold is used mainly to make jewellery.

## SUDBURY: FORESTRY AND MINING

**Population:** 85 354

**Transportation Routes:** road, rail, air (major airport)

**Location:** Northern Ontario

Sudbury is the largest city in northeastern Ontario. It is located at the spot where two highways and two railroads cross.

Sudbury is an important forestry and mining community. Its first nickel mine opened in 1888. By 1915, Sudbury's mines provided most of the world's nickel. The area is still one of the world's major sources of nickel. Other resources in the area include lead, zinc, silver, gold, cobalt, and platinum.

Sudbury is a major medical centre for its region. It is also the home of Laurentian University and Science North, a science museum.

## FOX LAKE RESERVE: FORESTRY

**Population:** 73

**Transportation Routes:** road, air (small airport in the nearby town of Chapleau)

**Location:** Northern Ontario

The Aboriginal people of Fox Lake Reserve are Cree. The modern community of Fox Lake began in 1989, although Aboriginal peoples have lived in this area for much longer. Like White River, the main industry here is forestry. Health and financial (such as banking) services are also important. On this reserve, people have jobs as nurses, accountants, secretaries, teachers, and railway and forestry workers.

The reserve also has a high-tech company, Cree-Tech Inc. It provides maps and other geographical information to governments and forestry companies across Canada. This company was founded and is managed by Aboriginal peoples.

*Wade Cachagee is president of Cree-Tech Inc., a high-tech company in the small community of Fox Lake Reserve. Are communities important because they are big? Or do other things make them important too?*

## GODERICH: MINING

**Population:** 7604

**Transportation Routes:** road, rail (freight—carrying goods only), water (major port and small craft), air (small airport)

**Location:** Southwestern Ontario

Goderich has a salt mine. Freighters (ships that carry goods) carry salt from Goderich to other parts of North America. The salt that is mined in Goderich is used mainly on roads in winter. Salt helps to melt ice, making roads less slippery.

Goderich also has a grain elevator. A **grain elevator** is a building where grain is collected and stored. The grain is then loaded onto boats, trains, or trucks.

Tourism is important in Goderich. Sandy beaches and nearby Point Farms Provincial Park and Falls Reserve Conservation Area attract tourists. Two local marinas (places where people can keep small private boats) attract boaters.

Other businesses in Goderich include a factory that makes large vehicles, such as road graders. Farming is also important in the area around Goderich.

*The town of Goderich is also called a port. It has a harbour where ships stop to load goods and take them to other places.*

### SOMETHING TO DO

1. White River and Fox Lake produce wood, Goderich produces road salt, and Sudbury produces nickel.

   a) With a partner, brainstorm how you use these resources in your community.

   b) What wood and paper products are used in your home, school, and community?

2. Do a class survey. Find out whose parents or guardians work in resource-based jobs (mining, farming, forestry, fishing) or in jobs related to manufacturing or selling these products. Whose parents or guardians work in jobs not related to resources (such as health care, education, banking)? Put your results in a bar graph.

3. Read a story about Winnie the Pooh by A.A. Milne. Imagine that Winnie comes back to Canada to visit White River or other communities. Write your own story or put on a play about Winnie.

**Dear Sintra and Kinzie,**

Did you know that, at one time in Ontario, most people were farmers and lived in rural communities? Today, most people in Ontario live in urban communities.

Growing crops and raising animals on farms is called **agriculture**. Few people in rural communities actually work on farms or are farmers. Still, it is an important industry. It gives us a safe and steady source of food. It also provides many jobs related to farms, from making butter to running restaurants or grocery stores.

The next time you go to a local grocery store, look to see how many things come from Canadian farms.

**Love,**
**Grandpa Shastri**

## QUICK DEFINITIONS

**Crops** are plants grown on farms, such as vegetables. Some crops are sold. Some are made into food, for people and for farm animals.

Pigs, chickens, turkeys, cattle, and sheep are called **livestock**. Farmers either sell their animals to be used as meat or sell the products from their animals (for example, milk from cows).

*During a drought, there is no rain for a long time. When this happens, plants dry up and die.*

What makes an area suitable for farming? Rich soil is one thing. Flat land or gently rolling hills that can be planted are another. Enough sunlight and rain are also needed for crops to grow.

Today, most farmers use large machines to do the work that many people and animals once did. Farmers need to know how to fix and take care of their machines. They must know how to look after their animals and crops. They also need to know how much to plant and when to **harvest** or gather the crops.

It is very expensive to start a farm today. Land, machines, seed for crops, and livestock all cost a lot of money. Many Ontario farms are still owned by families. People who own their own farms often have another job off the farm to earn enough for their families. Other farms are owned by companies. These are usually very large farms that do one type of farming.

Droughts, hailstorms, insects, diseases, and floods are all problems for farmers. Hail flattens crops so that they cannot be harvested. Some insects eat the crops. Diseases can kill both plants and animals. Major floods can drown plants. When there are several bad years in a row, some farmers cannot afford to keep their farms.

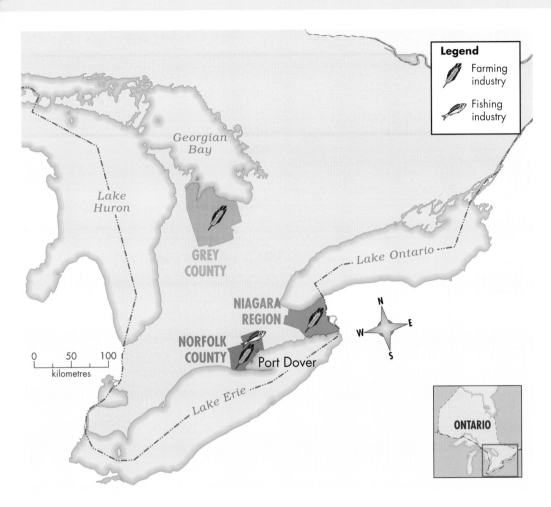

This map shows the locations of the farming and fishing communities discussed in this chapter.

**Legend**
- Farming industry
- Fishing industry

ONTARIO

## NIAGARA REGION: FARMING

**Population:** 410 000

**Transportation Routes:** road, ship (large and small), freight rail, airport (small)

**Location:** Southern Ontario

The Niagara region is excellent for farming because of its good weather and soil. The region is divided down the middle by the Niagara Escarpment.

On the Lake Ontario side of the Escarpment, the soil is deep, sandy, and very fertile. The Escarpment also protects farmland from harsh weather. The winters are shorter and less cold here. This makes the area ideal for growing many kinds of fruits and vegetables. These include grapes (for winemaking), cherries, plums, nectarines, and peaches.

Many farmers have begun growing plants, such as tomatoes, in greenhouses. **Greenhouses** are glass buildings. The glass walls and roofs keep the wind out and the heat in so that plants can be grown all year round.

There are also many urban communities in the Niagara region. These include St. Catharines, Niagara Falls, and Welland. Many tourists come to the Niagara region to see Niagara Falls. Some come to learn more about the history of the area. Tourists also tour fruit farms and wineries.

An **escarpment** is a long, steep ridge separating areas of land. The Niagara Escarpment runs across Ontario from Niagara Falls to Manitoulin Island.

## GREY COUNTY: FARMING

**Population:** 83 000

**Transportation Routes:** road, ship (small), airport (small)

**Location:** Southwestern Ontario

Farming is the main industry in Grey County because of its rich soil. The land in many parts is flat or has many small hills. There are more than 3000 farms in Grey County! It is the top producer of hay, apples, sheep, and lambs in Ontario. It is the second largest producer of cattle. Other types of farm products include barley, oats, wheat, corn, canola, honey, maple syrup, fruits and vegetables, pigs, goats, chickens, and turkeys.

Grey County also has an important tourist industry. The areas near Georgian Bay attract hikers, canoeists, and campers. In the winter, visitors come to places such as Blue Mountain to ski.

While much of Grey County is rural, there are some urban communities. These include the city of Owen Sound and the towns of Hanover, Meaford, Markdale, Flesherton, and Durham. These towns provide shopping, health care, and banking services to the nearby rural communities.

Many of these urban communities also have industries related to farming and tourism. Hanover has a flourmill. Markdale has an ice-cream factory. Owen Sound has stores that sell camping and boating equipment.

*Grey County has some untraditional farms. These include emu (shown here), buffalo, wild boar, and rare mushroom farms.*

## NORFOLK COUNTY: FARMING AND FISHING

**Population:** 60 000

**Transportation Routes:** road, ship, airport (small)

**Location:** Southern Ontario

Norfolk is an agricultural community on the shores of Lake Erie. Many areas there are flat and have rich soil. The main types of crops are corn, soybeans, rye, alfalfa, wheat, barley, oats, potatoes, and hay. There are some fruit and vegetable farms. Tobacco is also a common crop, but it is less important than it used to be because people now know that smoking tobacco causes cancer. Some farmers grow special crops, such as ginseng (a type of root), peanuts, garlic, mushrooms, sweet potatoes, herbs, and Christmas trees. Other farmers raise livestock.

Norfolk County has a number of small communities. One of these, Port Dover, is a fishing community with a harbour and beaches. In the past few years, there have been fewer fish because of overfishing.

**Overfishing** means catching more fish than nature can replace. To protect the fish, the government has made special rules about the kinds and number of fish that people can catch. Scientists hope that the number of fish will increase if fewer are caught. There will then be more fish that stay in the lake to breed for several years.

Port Dover is also a popular tourist spot in the summer months. People come here to swim, boat, and fish.

*At one time, Port Dover had one of the largest freshwater fishing businesses in Canada. The most common fish was lake perch.*

### SOMETHING TO DO

1. Make a collage to show the foods you eat that come from Canadian farms. You could use pictures from grocery-store flyers.

2. Make a class display of foods grown in your province. Bring packages (cans, boxes, labels) of three foods you like to eat that are grown or processed in your province. Make sure that the packages are clean! If the food is in season, bring a fresh sample to class.

3. What kinds of things do people farm? Research some different kinds of farms (dairy, beef, sheep, pigs, grains, vegetables, fruits, or fish). Pick one and make a map or model showing what foods or products might be made from the things these plants or animals give us.

**Dear Sintra and Kinzie,**

Each city is different, but one thing all cities have in common is that they have larger populations than the rural communities around them. Often, cities developed near important resources or along lakes and rivers that provided good transportation routes. Think about how the natural environment affected the development of these cities.

Love,
**Grandpa Shastri**

Many cities have some industry and manufacturing, stores, banks, government offices, hospitals, museums, theatres, sports arenas, and schools. The more people there are in a city, the more businesses and services are needed to serve them.

Big cities sometimes have big problems. For example, a big city has more traffic, more pollution, and more garbage than smaller communities. Can you think of other problems big cities might face?

Sometimes, cities grow very quickly. They start growing into lands needed by wildlife, forests, and farms. Careful planning by city planners, scientists, politicians, and citizens is needed to protect these lands from harmful development.

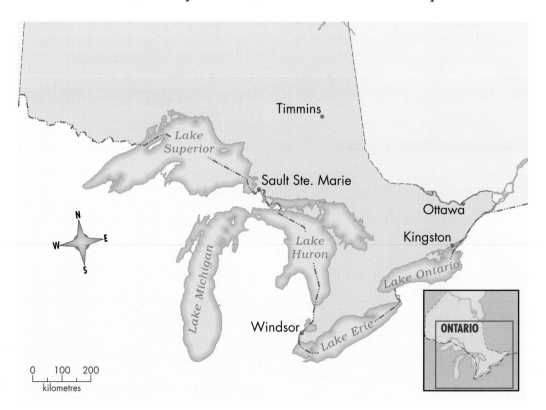

*This map shows the locations of the cities discussed in this chapter.*

## TIMMINS

**Population:** 43 686

**Land Area:** 2961 km²

**Transportation Routes:** road, air (major airport)

**Location:** Northern Ontario

The city of Timmins began in the early 1900s as a result of the Porcupine Gold Rush. During this time, many people explored the Porcupine area of Timmins, north of Porcupine Lake. They were looking for gold. Three main gold mines provided jobs for the community. Gold was transported by canoe and on foot until the railway arrived in 1911.

Since the early 1900s, zinc, silver, copper, and nickel mines have also been opened. Today, Timmins also has other industries, including forestry, manufacturing, technology, services, and tourism.

*During the Porcupine Gold Rush in the early 1900s, many people came to the Timmins area to look for gold.*

## SAULT STE. MARIE

**Population:** 74 566

**Land Area:** 223 km²

**Transportation Routes:** road, rail (freight), water (major port), air (major airport)

**Location:** Northern Ontario

The city of Sault Ste. Marie is often called the Soo. It has been an important trading and military community for a long time because of its location on St. Mary's River, which links Lake Superior and Lake Huron. The lakes provided a transportation route for shipping goods and military supplies. The city is also a key border crossing between Canada and the United States.

The people who live in the Soo work mostly in the steel, wood processing, pulp and paper, and transportation industries. Many services, such as hospitals and stores, serve a much larger area around Sault Ste. Marie.

## DID YOU KNOW?

Singer Shania Twain comes from Timmins, Ontario.

The first Canadian woman who travelled in space, Roberta Bondar, is from Sault Ste. Marie.

*The city of Sault Ste. Marie was named after the nearby falls on St. Mary's River. To help ships get around St. Mary's Falls, the city built **canals**—human-made waterways used for transportation.*

35

*The Ambassador Bridge is a suspension bridge. It is held up by strong cables attached to tall pillars at either end of the bridge.*

## WINDSOR

**Population:** 208 402

**Land Area:** 120 km²

**Transportation Routes:** road, rail (passenger and freight), water (major port and small craft), air (small airport)

**Location:** Southwestern Ontario

The city of Windsor is Canada's most southern city. It is an important border crossing into the United States. Detroit, Michigan, is just across the Detroit River from Windsor.

In the early 1900s, Windsor became the Canadian home for many car-making companies, including Ford, General Motors, and Chrysler. In addition to the auto industry, Windsor has construction, transportation, and service industries.

Windsor is home to the world's longest international suspension bridge—the Ambassador Bridge. It opened in 1929. Windsor also has the world's only international tunnel for cars and other vehicles. The Detroit–Windsor Auto Tunnel opened in 1930.

## KINGSTON

**Population:** 114 195

**Land Area:** 450 km²

**Transportation Routes:** road, rail (passenger), water (small craft), air (small airport)

**Location:** Eastern Ontario

The city of Kingston was the first capital of the United Province of Canada (now called Quebec and Ontario). It is home to many historical places, such as Canada's Royal Military College, Queen's University, and the Kingston Penitentiary.

Downtown Kingston is on Lake Ontario. It has many waterfront parks, water activities, and water sports. Many tourists come to explore the nearby Thousand Islands. Each year, sailors from around the world come to Kingston to sail their boats in the Canadian Olympic Training Regatta.

*The Royal Military College in Kingston*

### DID YOU KNOW?

The youngest prisoner in the Kingston Penitentiary was an 8-year-old, jailed for pickpocketing in 1845.

## OTTAWA

**Population:** 774 000

**Land Area:** 2778 km²

**Transportation Routes:** road, rail, air

**Location:** Eastern Ontario

Ottawa is Canada's capital. In the early 1800s, the most important industry in Ottawa was forestry. In 1867, it was chosen as the capital of the Dominion of Canada.

Once it became the capital, government became the most important business in Ottawa. This is where the prime minister lives. It is where people elected from across Canada meet in the parliament and make decisions about things like trade, natural resources, and the environment. Many people who live in Ottawa work for the government.

Tourism is also important to Ottawa—as many as 4 million people visit each year! People come to learn about how government works and to visit such places as the Canadian War Museum and the National Gallery. As well, Ottawa has a number of waterways, such as the Rideau River and the Ottawa River. Visitors there can enjoy going to the beach, boating, and playing water sports.

*The parliament buildings in Ottawa (left) are where our government makes decisions about our country. In the winter, visitors can skate on the nearby Rideau Canal (right), a part of the Rideau River, which links Ottawa to Lake Ontario.*

## SOMETHING TO DO

1. Look at the populations of each city in this section. List the cities in order from biggest to smallest population.

2. a) List the cities in order from biggest to smallest in land area. What do you notice about your list?

   b) Compare this list to your list of populations. Do the cities with the most population have the most land? Why do land area and population not go together?

3. a) Use a provincial road map. Locate all the cities from this section. Select three cities. Write a sentence telling what cardinal direction you would have to go from your community to this city.

   b) Write a sentence describing what method of transportation you could use to get to the city.

4. Research one of the cities in this section using library books or the Internet. (Many cities have good Web sites.) Find four or five new, interesting facts about this city, and write them down to share with your class.

## DID YOU KNOW?

The name Ottawa comes from the Algonquin word "adawe," which means "to trade." The Algonquin peoples once controlled trade on the Ottawa River.

**Dear Sintra and Kinzie,**

Did you know that the city of Toronto is actually part of a larger urban area called the Greater Toronto Area, or GTA? The GTA is huge and has many towns and cities within it. I'm sending you a map of the GTA and other information.

Why do you think the population in this area is so big? Why are there so many businesses and kinds of transportation here?

**Love,**
**Grandpa Shastri**

*This map shows the large city and four main regions that make up the GTA.*

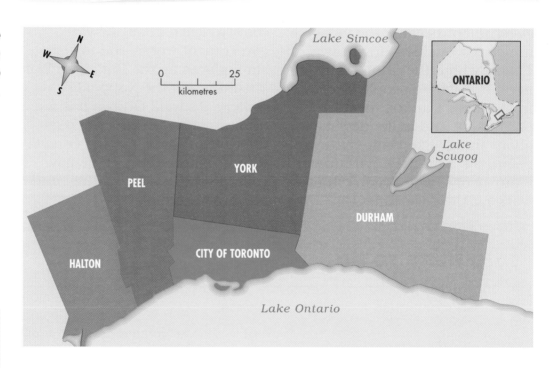

**DID YOU KNOW?**

The name Toronto means "Trees Standing in the Water" in Mohawk. More than 4.5 million people live in the GTA.

## WHAT IS THE GTA?

The GTA is in south central Canada. It is very close to the United States. It is made up of four regions—Durham, Peel, York, and Halton—and the city of Toronto. Each region is made up of smaller cities and towns. The GTA often seems like one giant city because many of its smaller cities have grown together and are connected. People in the GTA often live in one city and travel to work in another.

## HOW THE GTA GREW

Long before Europeans came to North America, the land around Toronto was part of a trail that Aboriginal peoples took between Lake Ontario and Lake Huron. In 1793, the British created the settlement of York. In 1834, the name York was changed to Toronto. In 1867, Toronto became the capital of the province of Ontario.

## Forests

In the early days, there were thick forests in the GTA. Settlers cleared trees, set up farms, and grew crops. The wood from trees was used to build homes and furniture. It was also used to heat homes.

## Land

The land around Toronto has rich, fertile soil. Plants grow well here. The climate is also good for plants. There is enough sun, rain, and warm temperatures. Some land in the GTA (such as the escarpment area near Milton) has steep hills, but most of it is flat with gentle, rolling hills. This is also important for farming.

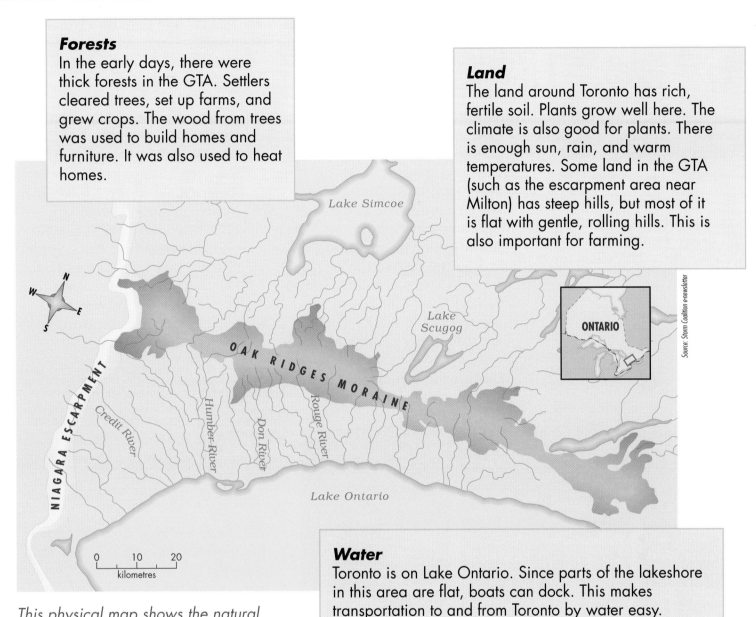

*Source: Storm Coalition e-newsletter*

*This physical map shows the natural features that helped the GTA to develop transportation, farming, and manufacturing.*

## Water

Toronto is on Lake Ontario. Since parts of the lakeshore in this area are flat, boats can dock. This makes transportation to and from Toronto by water easy.

In the early days, the many rivers in the GTA, such as the Humber, Credit, Don, and Rouge, provided water power to run machines at mills. Communities grew along these rivers. If you look at names of roads and communities in the GTA, you can see such names as Don Mills, York Mills, and Elgin Mills. These names show the early beginnings of these areas.

Communities in the GTA had many goods to trade because of the farms and mills in the area. Factories were built to produce goods. They also provided jobs. As more people moved here, more businesses came to the community. Settlers helped to build roads connecting the city of Toronto to other places in the province. Railways also helped to connect Toronto to the rest of Canada.

Less than 60 years ago, much of what is now the GTA was farmland with some small towns. These towns quickly grew and became large cities.

*The Toronto Pearson International Airport has grown even bigger in the last few years.*

*This map shows how the subway in the GTA is organized.*

## THE GTA TODAY

### Transportation

Today, much of the GTA's water and land are used for transportation.

- Lake Ontario still gives the people of the GTA an easy way to transport goods to other parts of Canada. The lake is connected to the St. Lawrence Seaway and the Atlantic Ocean, providing a link to the rest of the world.
- Toronto Pearson International Airport joins the GTA to the rest of the world. There are also many smaller airports within the GTA, such as Buttonville Airport and Toronto Island Airport.

- The GTA is joined to North America by passenger and freight rail links.
- Subway trains run underground and take people to many places within the city.
- Roads and highways join the GTA to the rest of North America.
- Many communities in the GTA have buses that people can ride to get around. Some of these are local buses that stay within each community. Others are GO buses that travel from one community in the GTA to another.

### Transportation Problems

With so many cars and trucks moving in the GTA, pollution has become a problem. Traffic jams at rush hour are also a problem.

Some ways to solve these problems are to

- add more subways and bus routes
- build apartments and houses near subways
- make more bicycle paths so fewer people need to drive

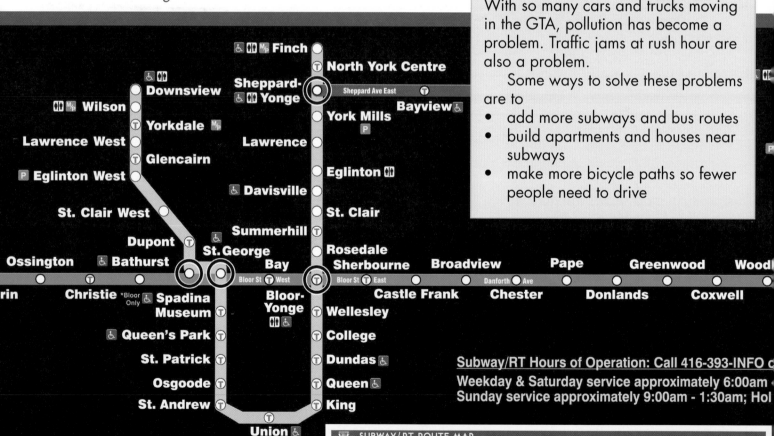

Source: Toronto Transit Commission © 2002

## Goods and Services

Toronto is the largest city in Canada. Most of Canada's big banks have their head offices here. While there are still some factories in Toronto, many have moved to other cities in the GTA, such as Brampton, Oshawa, Oakville, and Mississauga. Factories in the GTA produce everything from cars to clothing.

## Tourism and Culture

Tourism is an important industry in the GTA. The SkyDome and Air Canada Centre attract sports fans. Theatres bring in tourists from across North America. Museums and art galleries bring people who want to learn about the city and the world around them. While Toronto has many tourist sites, there are also others all over the rest of the GTA, such as Canada's Wonderland.

## THE FUTURE OF THE GTA

The GTA is growing even bigger. Many more people are now living in communities close to the city. The surrounding farmlands and rural communities are affected as the GTA spreads out onto these lands. People have to decide whether to protect land or use it for homes and businesses. Why is it important for people to plan how the land in the GTA will be used?

*A car plant in Oshawa. Why would this car plant be important for this community?*

*Caribana is one of many cultural celebrations in the GTA.*

*The Toronto Maple Leafs in action. Can you name three other professional sports teams based in Toronto?*

## SOMETHING TO DO

1. Examine the physical map of the GTA on page 39. List the important natural features it shows. Make a poster showing one of these features. Include a caption to explain how this feature has helped the GTA to grow.

2. Research an urban transportation system. You could use the subway map in this chapter (page 40), or you could get a map by visiting the Web sites for the Toronto Transit Commission, Mississauga Transit, Brampton Transit, York Region Transit, Ajax–Pickering Transit, or GO Transit.

   a) Make a list of the features in the legend. Describe how colour is used to help people read the information.

   b) Take a make-believe trip. Begin at the point farthest north on your map. Travel to the location that is farthest east. Make a list of the places you would travel through.

*Ping is Sintra's best friend. He and his mother are moving to Halifax. Ping has written a letter to Sintra and Kinzie to tell them why.*

# Dear Sintra and Kinzie,

My mom and I are here in Halifax for two weeks. We're here to find out more about the city before we move. You asked me why we're moving. I asked Mom the same question.

Mom says that the main reason we're moving is because she got a job here. Mom is a pediatrician (children's doctor). The hospital that she will be working at is big. People come to it from all over Atlantic Canada.

Mom said that one of the reasons she looked for a job in Halifax was that my grandparents live here. Mom lived in Halifax when she was growing up. Her parents came here from Hong Kong. She is excited about being closer to our relatives.

Halifax will be a good place to live. It will be great being so close to the ocean. We can walk along the waterfront and see the boats. There are many parks to walk and bike in. Mom says that the history of Halifax is interesting and we can learn about it at the museums.

Mom also likes Halifax because she could afford to buy a house here. Houses in Halifax cost less than houses in Toronto. Mom found a beautiful new house. There are many trees around it.

Mom won't have to drive to work every day. She can take a ferry across the harbour to get to work if she wants to.

There are some things we will miss. Mom will miss her friends in Toronto. I'll miss you. I'll also miss Dad because I won't be able to see him every weekend as I do now. But I will come back to Toronto to visit him at Christmas, at March break, and during the summer. I'll get to see you then. I'm a little scared about moving, but I'm also excited.

*Love,*
*Ping*

Halifax is the largest city in Atlantic Canada. Halifax is connected to the world by its port, where ships can load and unload goods and get repairs.

Many people in Halifax use buses and ferries to get around. Ferry service began in Halifax in 1752 and has continued for over 250 years.

Halifax is the capital of Nova Scotia. The province's government has its main offices here.

Many settlers of African ancestry came to Nova Scotia. They created an important African Canadian settlement in Halifax. The Black Cultural Centre helps to teach future generations about this history.

## SOMETHING TO DO

1. Work with a partner. In a web diagram, list the reasons that Ping's mother is moving to Halifax. Brainstorm other reasons, and add them to your web diagram.

2. Find out why your parents or guardians chose to live in your community. Write down their reasons. Compare them to the reasons Ping gives. Use a Venn diagram. Which reasons are the same? Which ones are different?

3. Create a poster showing a reason why people might choose to live in a community. You can look at Ping's reasons or at the reasons your family gave.

### DID YOU KNOW?

For thousands of years, Aboriginal peoples, such as the Mi'kmaq, lived along Nova Scotia's rivers and seacoasts. They hunted, fished, and used birchbark canoes for transportation. There are still Mi'kmaq and other Aboriginal communities in Nova Scotia today.

43

**Dear Sintra and Kinzie,**

Ontario is the province we live in. Your friend Ping has told you about moving to another province called Nova Scotia. Canada has ten provinces and three territories. Each province and territory has rural and urban communities. Each province and territory also has a capital city. Look at the map I am sending you to find the capital cities.

**Love,
Grandpa Shastri**

## DID YOU KNOW?

In 2002, Canada's population was just over 31 million. Over three-quarters of the people live in urban communities. The rest live in rural communities.

This map is a **political map**. It shows you the location of Canada's ten provinces and three territories, and their boundaries. **Provinces** and **territories** are the political areas into which Canada is divided. Look at the map legend. How are the boundaries between provinces and territories different from the boundary between countries?

Each province and territory has a **capital city** where its government is located. Toronto is the capital of Ontario. What symbol is used on the map to represent the capital cities of the provinces and territories? The map also shows Ottawa, the capital of Canada, where the country's government is located. How is the symbol used for Ottawa different from the symbol used for the other capital cities?

Governments provide many services to communities. The government of a province or territory takes care of services, such as health care, education, and transportation. The government of Canada looks after such things as trade with other countries and protection of this country with armed forces.

YUKON
TERRITORY

Whitehorse

NORTHW
TERRITO

Yellow

BRITISH
COLUMBIA

ALBERTA

Edmonton

*Pacific
Ocean*     Victoria

**Legend**
- – –   Border between provinces/territories
- ----   Border between countries
- ★   Capital of Canada
- ●   Capital of province/territory

## SOMETHING TO DO

1. a) Cover the names of the provinces, territories, and capitals on the map. With a partner, take turns naming the provinces, the territories, and their capital cities.

   b) Which province is farthest east? Which province is farthest west? Which capital city is farthest north?

2. Bring in maps to make a class collection. These might include street maps, road maps, bus-route maps, and maps of provincial parks or hiking trails. With a partner, pick a map from the collection. Study this map and make an oral presentation. Explain the following:

   a) What information can you find on the map?

   b) Where are the legend and symbols?

   c) How is colour used, and what does it show?

   d) Is this a map of an urban community, a rural community, or both?

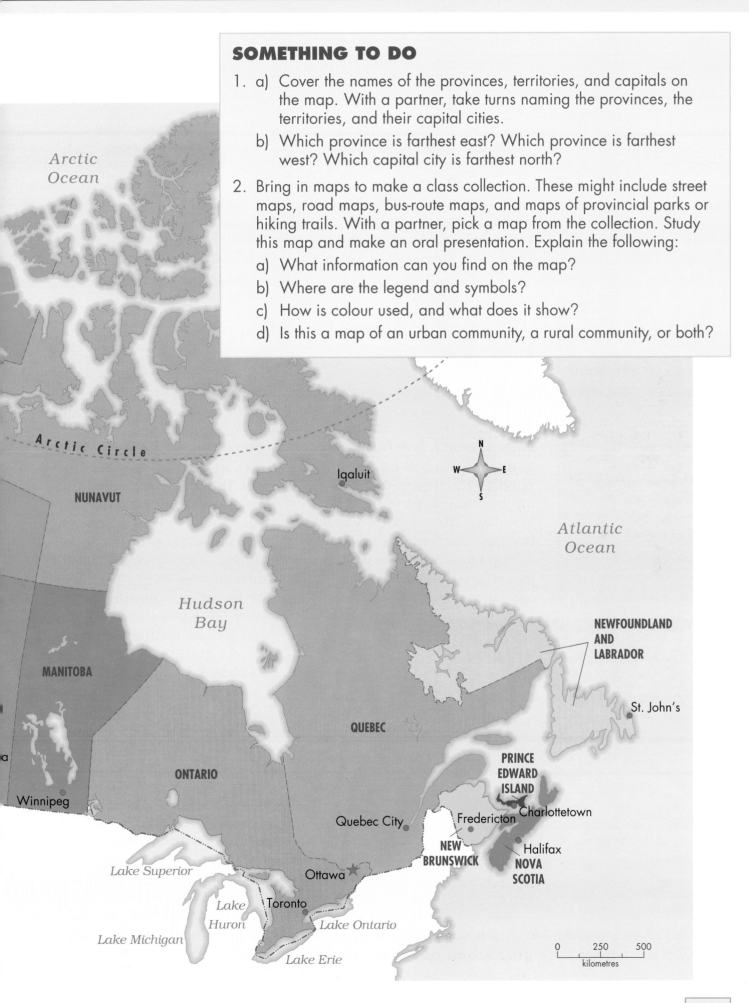

## 17

**Dear Sintra and Kinzie,**

I travel through some beautiful places in Ontario. When I'm in Toronto, I like to walk along the Don River. The Morris Tract near Goderich is also one of my favourite places. It is sad to think that some of these places may not stay beautiful and clean. We need to protect our environment. What do you think we can do to help?

Love,
Grandpa Shastri

## DID YOU KNOW?

When we throw paint cans or batteries into our garbage, harmful chemicals from them can leak out and damage the soil. Many communities have special programs to get rid of such items so that the environment won't be harmed.

## LAND PROBLEMS

### Farmland

As more people move into a city, more land is needed to build new homes, roads, and businesses. Many of Ontario's largest cities, such as Kitchener–Waterloo, are built on some of the best farmland. This causes a problem because farmers lose their way of making a living. As well, cities lose a local source of food.

### Forests

Sometimes, large parts of forests are cut down to build farms, roads, and homes for growing cities. Other times, logging companies cut down too many trees in the same area. Either way, natural homes of plants and animals, or **habitats**, are destroyed. It takes many years for trees to grow back. Some logging companies are now only cutting trees in certain parts of the forest and planting new trees. This helps to make sure that forests continue to grow.

### Garbage

Factories and people produce garbage. When there are more factories and people, there is more garbage. Garbage has become a big problem in many cities where they have run out of space at local dump sites. Some cities have started to move their garbage to dumps far away. For example, Toronto has taken a lot of its garbage to dumps in Michigan in the United States. Many rural and urban communities are working on projects to reduce the amount of garbage.

*One of the problems that cities have to deal with is garbage. What can happen when people throw garbage on city streets and sidewalks?*

## Pollution in the Soil

As cities grow, the number of factories also grows to make the goods that people need and want. Chemicals from factories can sometimes get into the soil on a piece of land. When this happens, people who live on this land or eat food grown on it can become sick. Today, there are laws about how factories should get rid of chemicals.

## WHAT YOU CAN DO

People in many cities are trying to clean up their environment and protect natural areas. One example of this is the cleanup of the Don River area in Toronto. On special cleanup days, hundreds of volunteers plant shrubs, trees, and wildflowers. They also help to clean up garbage and restore ponds and marshes.

In rural communities, people also try to protect their environment. An organization called the Nature Conservancy of Canada helps communities across Canada to buy and protect special land. In Huron County, near Goderich, the Nature Conservancy helped local people to save a piece of land called the Morris Tract.

*A cleanup day in the Don River area. This area is divided into two parts: one part is for public use, and the other part is protected for wildlife. How can you help to clean up or preserve natural areas in your community?*

*The Morris Tract is home to many old trees and rare plants as well as wildlife, such as birds, snakes, and frogs. Local people raised money to buy the land and create a protected park area.*

### SOMETHING TO DO

1. What parks are near your community? With a partner, create a web diagram. Show the things that you can do to help keep these parks clean and protect their wildlife.

2. What could you do to reduce garbage in your school? What could you do to make the natural environment around your school beautiful?

   With a partner, brainstorm your ideas. Create a brochure telling how you could help to keep your school and the natural environment around it beautiful.

**Dear Sintra and Kinzie,**

Thank you, Sintra, for your letter reminding me that we need to look after the air that we breathe. I know that this is important to you because of your asthma. You didn't enjoy last summer because of all the smog alerts about bad air. You had to stay indoors a lot. It is scary when it is hard to breathe on bad air days. We certainly need to look after the air in our communities.

**Love,
Grandpa Shastri**

---

**QUICK DEFINITION**

On some hot summer days, you can see a brown haze or fog. This is a type of air pollution called **smog**.

**DID YOU KNOW?**

Toronto, Mississauga, and Hamilton have the most serious problems with air pollution in the country. Air pollution is also spreading into rural communities.

## WHAT IS AIR POLLUTION?

Air pollution has been a big problem ever since people started to use coal, oil, and gas to run machines. Today we travel long distances quickly with cars and airplanes. We use lawn mowers to cut our grass and drive tractors on farmlands. Factories use coal to make electricity. But burning gas, oil, and coal give off harmful substances, which pollute our air.

### What Causes Air Pollution?

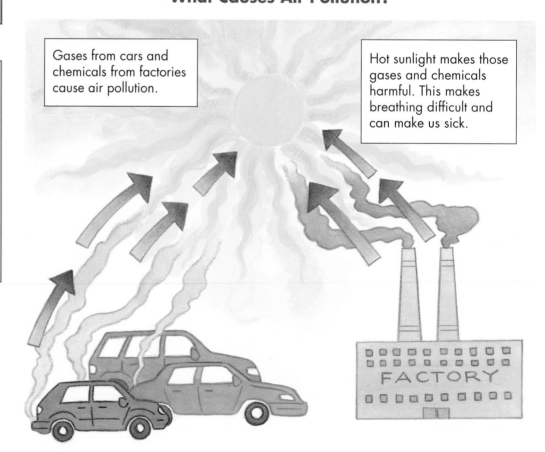

Gases from cars and chemicals from factories cause air pollution.

Hot sunlight makes those gases and chemicals harmful. This makes breathing difficult and can make us sick.

Some power plants in Ontario still use coal to make electricity. Many people have asked the provincial government to close coal-burning plants.

Coal is a hard, black rock. When it is burned, it pollutes the air.

## What Can I Do?

Here are some ways that you and your family can help reduce the amount of air pollution in your community:

- Walk as often as possible instead of going by car, especially when you are travelling short distances.
- Take the bus or subway rather than a car if you live in a large city.
- Use less electricity. Turn off lights and televisions when they are not needed.
- Encourage your family to rake leaves rather than use gas-burning tools like leaf blowers.
- Learn more about air pollution by reading about it.

## SOMETHING TO DO

1. Count the number of electrical outlets and light switches in your classroom and in your home. How many ways do you use electricity in a day? With a partner, brainstorm ways you could use less electricity. Make a brochure to show your good ideas.

2. Look at a catalogue or magazine. Cut out pictures of 20 to 30 small and large appliances. Sort them into two sections: things that make our lives easier and things that we could easily do without.

3. Make a mobile showing some of the ways you can help to reduce air pollution. Put your mobile up in your school.

Many scientists think that greenhouse gases (such as carbon dioxide) that cause air pollution are changing our climate. They believe that these gases are causing warmer temperatures, which melt snow. This, in turn, causes floods.

**Dear Sintra and Kinzie,**

Thank you, Kinzie, for your letter telling me how important water is to communities. I know you are aware of this because Hanover is very close to Walkerton. There was a problem with the drinking water in Walkerton a few years ago. Many people became sick. Some people even died.

People all over Canada raised money to try to help. That is one of the good things about communities—when one community has a problem, others try to help.

**Love,
Grandpa Shastri**

## USES OF WATER

### Transportation

Water has always been an important means of transportation in Ontario. Ships can carry goods on the St. Lawrence Seaway and the Great Lakes. Ships carry bigger loads and need less fuel than airplanes. It is cheaper to move goods by ship.

### Recreation

Many rural and urban communities use their rivers and lakes for recreation. Communities along the Trent–Severn Waterway and along lakes in Muskoka have created resorts, parks, and businesses that offer water sports, such as canoeing and fishing.

### Drinking and Washing

All communities need drinking water. In some rural communities, homeowners own and take care of their own **wells**. These are holes dug deep into the ground where there are large pockets of water. This **groundwater** is between layers of clay, rock, and soil. Pipes from a well connect to sinks, tubs, toilets, and taps in the house.

In urban communities, water resources are usually shared. Both the town or city government and the provincial government look after the water resources. People pay for the water they use.

Towns and cities get their water from different sources. Some communities get their drinking water directly from lakes and rivers. Others that are not near lakes or rivers have large wells that collect groundwater. Some communities build **reservoirs**. These are artificial ponds that collect rainwater for later use. The water is cleaned and then piped to homes and other buildings.

*Why do we need to drink water?*

## A Water Filtration System

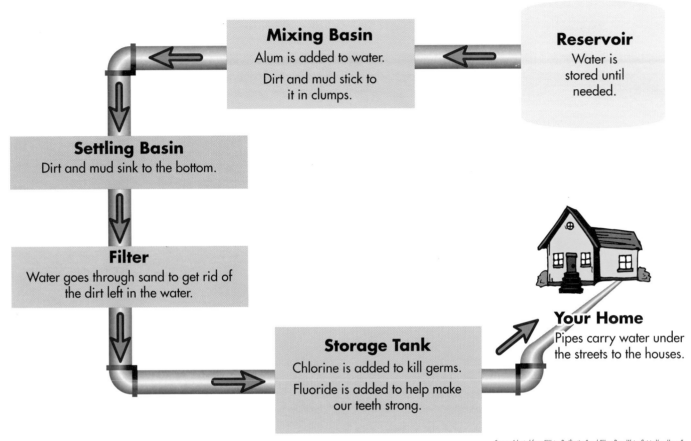

**Mixing Basin**
Alum is added to water.
Dirt and mud stick to it in clumps.

**Reservoir**
Water is stored until needed.

**Settling Basin**
Dirt and mud sink to the bottom.

**Filter**
Water goes through sand to get rid of the dirt left in the water.

**Storage Tank**
Chlorine is added to kill germs.
Fluoride is added to help make our teeth strong.

**Your Home**
Pipes carry water under the streets to the houses.

*Source: Adapted from "Water Purification" and "How Does Water Get to Your House",*
*Water (Science Works for Kids Series), pp. 70–71, © by Evan-Moor Corp.*

## WATER PROBLEMS

### Bacteria
**Bacteria** are very tiny living things that can be seen only through a microscope. Some bacteria can cause disease. When harmful bacteria get into lakes, people should not swim in them. Beaches in large cities are often closed during the summer because of bacteria in the water.

It is even more serious when harmful bacteria get into drinking water. Harmful bacteria can enter our drinking water through **sewers** (large underground pipes) that connect our towns and cities to lakes and rivers. In rural communities, runoff from manure, or cattle waste, in farms sometimes washes into wells and rivers.

### Walkerton—A Canadian Water Crisis
It is a serious problem when our water is unsafe for drinking. In the spring of 2000 in Walkerton, Ontario, a heavy rainfall washed a harmful type of bacteria, called E. coli, into one of the town's wells. People were not told of the problem in time. Seven people died and 2300 became sick. Many of the people who got sick still have health problems. Some of them will have health problems for the rest of their lives. It was many months before the people in Walkerton could use the water from their taps again.

*Water is stored in the Walkerton water tower.*

**Acid Rain**

## How Acid Rain Is Formed

Sulphur from factories

Sulphur from chemicals

Sulphur from car exhaust

1. **Acid rain** is a type of pollution. A chemical called sulphur enters the atmosphere and makes acid rain.

2. Acid rain leaves the atmosphere as rain and snow.

3. Acid rain looks and smells clean. Over time, though, it causes a lot of damage to lakes, rivers, forests, animals, and plants.

*Source: Acid Rain Retirement Fund website*

## DID YOU KNOW?

Vinegar is an acid. It is mild and safe for human use. Some stronger acids can burn skin. Like vinegar, acid rain is mild enough not to hurt people. Unfortunately, over time it can hurt plants and animals. One kind of tree harmed by acid rain is the sugar maple.

## How Can We Help?

Canada has a lot of clean water, and it is usually safe. The more water we have, the more we use. That is a problem. Many countries don't have the amount of water that we do. Only 3 per cent of the world's water is fresh water that is safe for drinking. If you filled a cup with 100 marbles and picked out 3, that would show you how much of the world's water we could actually use to drink! How can you conserve water? Are there ways you could use less?

## SOMETHING TO DO

1. Get two small plants. Water one with ordinary tap water. Water the other with vinegar. Watch what happens and record it in a journal over several weeks. What does this tell you about the effects of acid rain on forests and lakes?

2. We sometimes forget just how important water is and how often we use it. Record all the times you use water in a day using a tally. Mark every time you use water (such as for drinking, washing hands, showering, flushing a toilet, or cooking).

3. Fill up a two-litre pop bottle. In some parts of the world, this is all the water people have for a day. How would your life change if this were all the water you had for a whole day?

**Dear Sintra and Kinzie,**

I'm glad to hear that you are planting gardens this year. Kinzie, I know that yours will be in your own backyard. Sintra, you are going to use an allotment garden near your home. What a great idea! I can hardly wait to taste the food you grow later this year.

Remember that there are many things you can do to help the environment in your own backyards. "Backyard" can mean our community as well as our own property.

**Love,
Grandpa Shastri**

## GARDENING

Gardening means growing plants outdoors or in a greenhouse. Plants are good for the environment because they put back nutrients into the soil and clean the air. People can grow fruits, vegetables, and flowers in their gardens. Some people like growing **organic food** in their gardens. This type of food is grown without using any chemicals.

Even if you live in an apartment, you can grow a few vegetables, such as tomatoes, in a container. Having a garden can be fun. You may not grow enough food to feed your family, but you will learn a lot about what it takes to help plants grow. The results are often tasty!

## CHEMICALS WE USE

During the early days of farming, insects and disease often ruined foods growing in fields and gardens. Scientists began to develop chemicals to kill insects and prevent disease.

Unfortunately, these scientists did not always know that some of the chemicals were harmful to the environment. A chemical called DDT was used. People discovered that it was entering the environment through water and soil. It was killing some birds and causing cancer in some humans.

Many people are worried about chemicals, especially those used to make our lawns greener. Many rural and urban communities in Canada have laws about what people can and cannot spray on their property. Some places are trying to ban chemical spraying altogether.

## REDUCING, REUSING, RECYCLING

One way to help our environment is to reduce, or cut down, the amount of garbage we create. The more packaging a product has, the more garbage it creates. Buy products with as little packaging as possible. When there is less garbage to get rid of, all communities benefit.

People who do not have enough land for a garden can rent a small plot to grow vegetables or flowers. This plot of land is an **allotment garden**.

*Some things you can compost are fruit and vegetable peels, tea bags, coffee grounds, eggshells, grass clippings, leaves, and weeds.*

Another way is to reuse things. When you give your used clothing or toys to younger brothers, sisters, or friends (or when they give items to you), you are reusing them. When we reuse things, we don't need to use as many new resources. Reusing can also save your family money!

**Recycling** means taking things we no longer want and turning them into new products. When we recycle, the old object is usually broken down and made into a new one. For example, old pop cans can be melted down at factories and made into new ones. You can also recycle when you make something new, such as a pencil holder, out of something old, such as a milk carton. When we recycle, we create less garbage.

## COMPOSTING

**Composting** is a special kind of recycling. It means collecting dead plants and other things that rot easily to create **fertilizer**. This fertilizer can be added to the soil to give food to the plants. When we compost, less waste goes into our garbage and then on to dumps.

Composting is good for the environment no matter where you live. It is especially important in cities where there are so many people. Think about how much more garbage there would be if people did not compost!

### You Can Make a Difference!

- Make a garden in your backyard (even if your backyard is the balcony of an apartment).
- Help with a tree-planting project.
- Help to clean up a local park or river.
- Throw your waste in a garbage can, not on the ground.
- Buy things with less packaging.
- Recycle your cans, paper, and glass.
- Write to toy companies or fast-food restaurants that use a lot of plastic and cardboard wrapping. Ask them to use less packaging.
- Give away old clothes and toys to family, friends, and homeless people's shelters instead of throwing them away.
- Read about the environment and learn about ways to protect it.

### SOMETHING TO DO

1. Track your classroom's garbage for a week. Keep a clipboard beside all garbage cans in the room. Each time you throw something into a garbage can, write down what it is.

   At the end of the week, read over the list. As a class, make a circle graph of the five things that are most often thrown out. Discuss how you could cut down on garbage.

2. Recycle some things. Bring in boxes, paper-towel rolls, cans, plastic tubs, and milk and egg cartons. Create a useful object. Write out the instructions for making your object, and share them with your classmates.

After Sintra and Kinzie visited each other, they each wrote a report about the time that they spent together. Read their reports. Ask yourself these questions: How are rural and urban communities alike? How are they different? How are communities connected?

## SINTRA'S REPORT

We were very excited about Kinzie and her family's visit to Toronto!

**Sunday**

P.M.: Kinzie and her family drove up to our house. After they unpacked, we played in Taylor Creek Park. Then we took a walk around my neighbourhood. Kinzie said that the houses are much closer together here than on her street. We walked to the Danforth and looked at the stores. Kinzie saw that the street signs are in Greek and English. We bought Italian ice cream called gelato at a restaurant. It was nice and cold!

**Monday**

A.M.: After breakfast, we walked to the subway and took it downtown to the CN Tower. It was fun going up the elevator on the side of the tower. My mom used to have a teacher who would walk up the stairs of the CN Tower once a year to raise money for charity. The observation deck was cool. You could see the whole city through binoculars. There were so many roads, factories, and buildings! It looked like a giant map.

P.M.: For lunch, we had dim sum at one of my favourite restaurants in Chinatown. We tasted many different foods that came in small dishes. Our favourite was har guun. It's a deep-fried roll filled with shrimp. It was yummy!

Many people who live in the community around Danforth Avenue have Greek heritage. To celebrate this, many street signs on the Danforth are written in both English and Greek.

At Chinese dim sum, servers roll around carts with lots of delicious food on them.

*The Beaches in Toronto*

*Musicians play music at Harbourfront.*

*Zoos help us to learn about nature and protecting our environment.*

## Tuesday

**A.M.:** We strolled down the boardwalk in the Beaches. The Beaches is on Lake Ontario. We saw dogs playing in the lake. We also saw some windsurfers. There were lots of people jogging, rollerblading, and biking. We played on the swings and went for a swim in the Olympic pool.

**P.M.:** We went to the Walter Stewart Library. It was the day for "Reading Around the World." This is a special reading program being used at libraries all over Ontario this summer. Kinzie said that they have it at her library in Hanover, too! We watched Hilary, the librarian, do a puppet play about a Caribbean Anansi story. Then we did crafts.

## Wednesday

**ALL DAY!** Today we went to Centre Island, one of my favourite places! We packed a picnic lunch and took the ferry across the lake to the island. We walked around and looked at the boats on the water and the Canada geese. We went on lots of rides at Centreville! It was so much fun going down the log ride and splashing in the water.

**LATE P.M.:** My dad played a concert with his jazz band at Harbourfront. Many of my friends and family came to the concert. Kinzie's parents got to see friends and family they had not seen in a long time.

## Thursday

We went to our friend Ping's apartment. He lives in a high-rise building with a pool. Ping's mom took us to the Royal Ontario Museum. It is huge! We had a lot of fun exploring the bat cave. We also dug for dinosaur bones in the sand. That was great!

## Friday

**ALL DAY!** We went to the Toronto Zoo. I wanted to see the Komodo dragon, Kinzie wanted to see Siberian tigers, Kaye wanted to see the polar bears, and Joseph wanted to see the gorillas. We even went for a camel ride and played in the splash park to cool off. We stopped by a Trinidadian restaurant on the Danforth for chicken roti and coconut water. I love chicken roti. It's like a chicken wrap but has potato and spices too. Our parents were so tired at the end of the day!

**Saturday**

**A.M.:** We went to my school playground to play. Then we went back home so Kinzie could finish packing. We were sad that the week was over. Kinzie and her family were leaving in the afternoon. We are looking forward to seeing them in Grey County in a few weeks.

# KINZIE'S REPORT

It was great having Sintra and her family visit us!

**Sunday**

**P.M.:** Sintra and her family arrived by car. Sintra noticed that our yard is much bigger than hers. We all walked down to the lake for canoeing. We put on our life jackets and took turns going out on the lake with Dad. Sintra and I pretended we were explorers.

**Monday**

**A.M.:** After breakfast, Sintra and I walked down the road to visit my neighbours. They live on a dairy farm. Steve is also 8 years old. We take the bus to school together. In the summer, his 14-year-old stepsister, Erin, comes to visit from Thunder Bay. She helps to look after him. Steve's mom took us to the barn and showed us the milking machines and how they work. Later, Steve's dad had to go cut his hayfield. We played outside. At lunchtime, we walked to the field to give Steve's dad his lunch.

**P.M.:** After lunch, Steve's mom drove us to Chesley. It takes about 10 minutes to get there by car. There is a new water park in Chesley. We played under the giant sprinklers for a long time.

**Tuesday**

**A.M.:** We went for a walk along the community hiking trails in Hanover with my mom. In one place, there is a huge elm tree that is almost 300 years old! Last year, my school had a special Earth Day celebration there. I showed the tree to Sintra. She thought it was amazing. We had a picnic lunch by the tree.

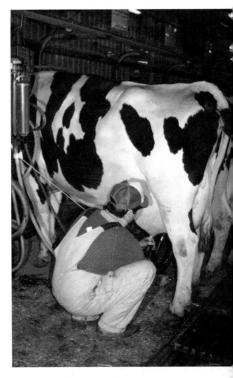

*Steve's dad milks cows on his farm.*

*Earth Day celebrations on the community hiking trails.*

P.M.: Tonight we had a campfire in our yard. We cooked some hot dogs over the fire. We put up tents and slept outside. The stars were beautiful. We could hear the crickets—and Steve's dad's tractor!

### Wednesday

A.M.: Today it rained. That was OK. The farmers need rain for the crops to grow. We went to the library. Bill, the librarian, told us a story about a Chinese dragon. Then we played a quiz game about places around the world.

P.M.: After lunch, my dad took us to his clinic. He works with two other vets. They often visit farms to help cows, pigs, horses, sheep, and goats. They also spend time at their office seeing pets like dogs and cats.

### Thursday

A.M.: It stopped raining! We built a tree fort in the backyard. Mom took us to the Saugeen Municipal Airport for lunch. We met some pilots she works with, and we watched the planes take off and land.

P.M.: Our parents took us swimming at the Hanover Aquatic Centre. It has two indoor pools. One has a huge waterslide.

### Friday

A.M.: Today our parents drove us to Goderich to swim at the beach and visit my grandma. Goderich is about an hour away and is on the shore of Lake Huron. Grandma lives in a big house on a hill overlooking Lake Huron and the Maitland River. Her house is on land that her great-grandparents used to farm. Now a neighbour farms the land.

P.M.: Grandma took us to the Huron County Museum. There is one section that is like a store from long ago. There was also a special fossil display on loan from the ROM in Toronto! For supper, we went back to the beach and bought fish and chips. At sunset, the Goderich Pipe Band played their bagpipes.

### Saturday

A.M.: It's hard to believe that our week is over! We took the canoe out on the lake again. I've already started thinking about some of the things I'd like to do next time—maybe look for fossils along the Saugeen River.

*Every summer, libraries all over Ontario have special kids' programs. This year, the theme is "Reading Around the World."*

*This beach at Goderich is part of the natural environment.*

# Comparing Our Communities

## Comparing Kinzie and Sintra's Communities

### Sintra's Urban Community
- Busy roads (all paved)
- Many kinds of homes built close together (single-family houses, duplexes, townhouses, apartments)
- Many people and buildings
- Sounds of traffic, sirens, and people playing
- Small yards
- Subways, public buses, and cars used to get around
- Many museums
- Offices, stores, factories, and hospitals where people work

### Both
- Roads
- Lakes nearby
- Nice parks
- Libraries
- Swimming pools
- Schools
- Hospitals, police force, and firefighting services

### Kinzie's Rural Community
- Quiet roads (some paved, some gravel or dirt)
- Single-family houses built far apart
- Many fields and farms
- Sounds of farm machinery and animals
- Large yards
- Cars and school buses used to get around
- Stores, farms, and seniors' homes where people work

*Consider Kinzie and Sintra's visits. In what other ways were they the same? How else were they different?*

## STEREOTYPES ABOUT URBAN AND RURAL PEOPLE

Sometimes people have certain ideas about a type of person. These ideas may not be true. We call such a general idea a **stereotype**.

Some city people have stereotypes about rural people. They see rural people as having little culture. Some rural people have stereotypes about city people. They think that city people are unfriendly and don't know their neighbours.

The truth is that many rural people are interested in cultural events. Like urban people, many rural people go to concerts and plays. There are many summer theatre festivals in small towns and cities, such as Stratford, Blyth, and Collingwood. Many city people are friendly and do know their neighbours. Like rural people, many meet at local community centres, libraries, parks, schools, places of worship, and clubs.

Rural and urban people have many things in common. Both rural and urban communities can be good places to live.

*Sintra, Kinzie, and their families had a great time on their visits. These families have many things in common.*

## SOMETHING TO DO: YOUR COMMUNITY

This last chapter is one that you can add to! It's your turn to write about the place where you live. Look at our report for the made-up community "Goodplace" below.

1. There are 13 statements to complete in this report. Copy them onto lined paper, and write answers about your own community.
2. Draw a map and some pictures of your community.
3. Compare your community to either Sintra's or Kinzie's community, whichever is more different.

My community is
Goodplace in southeastern Ontario.

The natural environment affects my community because
Goodplace is on Lake Ontario so people fish and use the lake for recreation. The land has small hills and flat areas with good soil. This allows people to farm.

It is a rural/(urban) community.
It is a medium-sized urban community (a town) with rural land all around it.

The population is
11 000.

Jobs people have in this community are
selling farm machinery and working at a small cheese factory, at a local grain mill, at a local food-processing plant, at a local clothing factory, in jobs related to tourism, and in stores.

Some services that are important for my family include
a hospital, Goodplace Police, Goodplace Fire Department, six schools, a library, many stores on the main street, and two malls.

You can get around by
car, bike, small boat, and buses that go to Ottawa and Toronto four times a week.

If friends came to visit me, I would want to take them to see the beach at Lake Ontario. We could also visit my school. We could watch the local baseball and hockey teams play. We could hike on nature trails in the parks nearby. We could visit the pioneer museum.

Places in my community for recreation are a beach, an indoor pool, and the local arena for hockey, skating, and curling. There is a marina for boats. Two parks in town have playgrounds, baseball diamonds, and soccer fields. A provincial park just outside town has hiking and skiing trails.

Some special cultural events in my community are the Big Race in July (when people come from all over the province to race their canoes), the Concert in the Barn, and the Powwow (where Aboriginal peoples in our area celebrate and teach us about their culture).

We look after the environment in my community by recycling, cleaning up litter at the park and beach, and not wasting water.

Some good things about my community are that it is safe and the people are friendly. A famous hockey player called Ted Goodshot came from our city.

Two things I would like to change about my community are its library and its hospital. I would like to make our library bigger (some grown-ups have started a campaign to do this). I would like to have more doctors at our hospital.

# Glossary

**acid rain** a type of pollution that gets into our environment from car exhaust, factory smokestacks, and chemicals that we spray on lawns and farms.

**agricultural land** land used for farming.

**agriculture** the growing of crops and raising of animals in farming.

**allotment garden** a place where people who don't have enough land to garden can rent space.

**ancestry** the people from whom you are descended, such as grandparents.

**bacteria** very tiny living things that can be seen only through a microscope. Some bacteria can cause disease.

**barter system** the system of trading some goods (such as corn) for other goods (such as a canoe).

**canal** a human-made waterway used for transportation.

**capital city** the location of the government for a political area, such as a province, territory, or country.

**cardinal points** the four main points of the compass—north, south, east, and west.

**city** a large urban community.

**commercial land** land that is used for stores and offices.

**community** a group of people who share common interests and experiences. They often live or work in the same area.

**compass rose** the symbol on a map that shows the directions north, south, east, and west.

**composting** a kind of recycling that involves collecting dead plants and other things that rot easily, such as eggshells, to create new soil.

**consumer** someone who buys goods and services.

**coordinate** the number and letter on a grid that we use together to locate a place.

**crops** the plants grown on farms, such as fruits, vegetables, and grains.

**culture** people's beliefs and the way they live their lives, including their clothing, food, celebrations, languages, and music.

**environment** the air, water, and land around us.

**escarpment** a long, steep ridge separating areas of land at different heights.

**exporting** the selling of goods or services to other provinces, territories, or countries.

**factory** a place where goods are processed or manufactured.

**fertilizers** materials added to the soil to enrich it and help plants and crops grow.

**filtration system** a system that helps communities clean the water they use. This system is normally housed in a building called a filtration plant.

**forestry** the planting and harvesting of trees to create wood products, such as paper, boards, or furniture.

**goods** products that are produced or manufactured, such as food, clothing, and books.

**grain elevator** a building where grain is collected and stored and then loaded onto boats, trains, or trucks.

**greenhouses** glass buildings used for growing plants all year round.

**grid** a pattern of horizontal and vertical lines on a map used to locate places.

**groundwater** large pockets of water deep underground within layers of clay, rock, and soil.

**habitats** the natural homes of plants and animals.

**hamlet** a group of houses in a rural community, smaller than a village.

**harvest** to gather in crops when they are ready or ripe.

**heritage** everything that has been handed down from the past, such as stories, music, and ways of preparing food.

**importing** the buying of goods and services from other provinces, territories, or countries.

**industrial buildings** buildings where goods are processed or manufactured, such as factories.

**industry** the business of processing or manufacturing goods.

**institutional buildings** public buildings, such as schools, hospitals, and places of worship.

**legend** a list explaining the symbols found on a map.

**legends** true or fictional stories passed down from one generation to the next.

**livestock** the animals raised on a farm, such as pigs, chickens, turkeys, cattle, goats, and sheep.

**manufacturing** the process of changing resources into items that people use.

**mills** buildings with machinery for manufacturing goods, such as machines to grind grains to make flour.

**minerals** natural resources that are found in rocks, such as nickel and gold.

**mining** the process of digging into the ground using machines to find minerals.

**natural resources** things produced by nature that are useful to people, such as trees or minerals.

**organic food** food that is grown without using any chemicals.

**overfishing** catching more fish than nature can replace.

**physical features** hills, valleys, rivers, lakes, and other natural forms that make up an environment.

**physical maps** maps that show what the land looks like.

**political maps** maps that show boundary lines between political areas, such as provinces, territories, and countries.

**population** the number of people living in an area or community.

**port** a place where ships can load and unload goods.

**processing** the process of changing crops or resources into food or things that people use.

**provinces** some of the political areas into which Canada is divided.

**recreation** an activity done for fun, such as walking, swimming, skiing, canoeing, or camping.

**recycling** taking materials we no longer want and turning them into new products.

**reserve** a piece of land set aside by the government for Aboriginal peoples.

**reservoirs** artificial ponds that collect rainwater for later use.

**residential land** land used for housing.

**road maps** maps that show major roads, highways, and other transportation routes to help us find out how to get from one place to another.

**rural community** a group of people outside an urban community who live spread out over a large area.

**scale** the bar on a map that looks like a ruler and tells you the real size of things and the real distances.

**services** things people do for others in communities. For example, mail carriers provide the service of delivering our mail.

**sewers** large underground pipes that take the waste water out of people's houses and other buildings. Sewers also direct street runoff from rain and snow away from roads and homes to prevent flooding.

**smelting** the process of separating minerals from rocks using high heat.

**smog** a type of air pollution that causes a brown haze or fog on some hot summer days.

**stereotype** a general idea we may have about a type of person. This idea may not be true.

**street maps** maps that help us to find such things as town or city streets, schools, hospitals, parks, and shopping malls.

# Glossary

**symbol** a picture, colour, shape, or line on a map that stands for something, such as a road, a building, or water.

**territories** some of the political areas into which Canada is divided.

**tourism** a business that helps people who are visiting a community.

**tourists** people who travel to other places to visit and spend their holidays.

**town** a small urban community.

**trade** the buying or selling of goods and services.

**traditions** the ideas and ways of doing things that are passed on to younger generations.

**transportation routes** the roads, railroad lines, lakes, and rivers that can be used to move goods and people from one place to another.

**urban community** a group of many people living close together. Towns and cities are urban communities.

**village** a rural community that is larger than a hamlet but smaller than a town.

**wells** holes dug deep into the ground to find large pockets of water.